TEACHING
SELF-DEFENSE

Steps to Success

Joan M. Nelson, MA
Founder/Director, Movement Arts, Inc.
Lansing, Michigan

Human Kinetics Publishers

Library of Congress Cataloging-in-Publication Data

Nelson, Joan M., 1949-
    Teaching self-defense : steps to success / Joan M. Nelson.
        p. cm.
    ISBN 0-87322-620-8
    1. Self-defense--Study and teaching.   I. Title.
    GV1111.N46   1994
    613.6'6--dc20   93-31620
                                             CIP

ISBN: 0-87322-620-8

Acquisitions Editor: Brian Holding; **Developmental Editor:** Rodd Whelpley; **Assistant Editors:** Sally Bayless, Moyra Knight, Lisa Sotirelis; **Copyeditor:** Dianna Matlosz; **Proofreader:** Dawn Barker; **Production Director:** Ernie Noa; **Typesetter:** Ruby Zimmerman; **Text Layout:** Tara Welsch; **Text Design:** Keith Blomberg; **Cover Design:** Jack Davis; **Cover Photo:** Wilmer Zehr; **Mac Diagrams:** Gretchen Walters; **Line Drawings:** Tim Offenstein; **Printer:** United Graphics

Instructional Designer for the Steps to Success Activity Series: Joan N. Vickers, EdD, University of Calgary, Calgary, Alberta, Canada

Human Kinetics books are available at special discounts for bulk purchase for sales promotions, premiums, fundraising, or educational use. Special editions or book excerpts can also be created to specification. For details, contact the Special Sales Manager at Human Kinetics.

Printed in the United States of America

10 9 8 7 6 5 4 3 2 1

Human Kinetics Publishers
Box 5076, Champaign, IL 61825-5076
1-800-747-4457

Canada: Human Kinetics Publishers, Box 24040, Windsor, ON N8Y 4Y9
1-800-465-7301 (in Canada only)

Europe: Human Kinetics Publishers (Europe) Ltd., P.O. Box IW14, Leeds LS16 6TR, England
0532-781708

Australia: Human Kinetics Publishers, P.O. Box 80, Kingswood 5062, South Australia
618-374-0433

New Zealand: Human Kinetics Publishers, P.O. Box 105-231, Auckland 1
(09) 309-2259

Contents

Series Preface

The Steps to Success Activity Series is a breakthrough in skill instruction through the development of complete learning progressions—the *steps to success*. These *steps* help individuals quickly perform basic skills successfully and prepare them to acquire more advanced skills readily. At each step, individuals are encouraged to learn at their own pace and to integrate their new skills into the total action of the activity.

The unique features of the Steps to Success Activity Series are the result of comprehensive development—through analyzing existing activity books, incorporating the latest research from the sport sciences, and consulting with students, instructors, teacher educators, and administrators. This groundwork pointed up the need for three different types of books—for participants, instructors, and teacher educators—which we have created and which together comprise the Steps to Success Activity Series.

The participant's book, *Self-Defense: Steps to Success*, is a self-paced, step-by-step guide that you can use as an instructional tool. The unique features of the participant's book include

- sequential illustrations that clearly show proper technique,
- helpful suggestions for detecting and correcting errors,
- excellent practice progressions with accompanying Success Goals for measuring performance, and
- checklists for rating technique.

A comprehensive instructor's guide, *Teaching Self-Defense: Steps to Success*, accompanies the participant's book. This instructor's guide emphasizes how to individualize instruction. Each step of this instructor's guide promotes successful teaching and learning with

- teaching cues (Student Keys to Success) that emphasize fluidity, rhythm, and wholeness,
- criterion-referenced rating charts for evaluating a participant's initial skill level,
- suggestions for observing and correcting typical errors,
- tips for group management and safety,

- ideas for modifying the difficulty level,
- quantitative evaluations for all drills (Success Goals), and
- a test bank of written questions.

The series textbook, *Instructional Design for Teaching Physical Activities* (Vickers, 1990), explains the *steps to success* model, which is the basis for the Steps to Success Activity Series. Teacher educators can use the series textbook in their professional preparation classes to help future teachers and coaches learn how to design effective physical activity programs in school, recreation, or community teaching and coaching settings.

After identifying the need for various texts, we refined the *steps to success* instructional design model and developed prototypes. Once these prototypes were fine-tuned, we carefully selected authors for the activities who were not only thoroughly familiar with their sports but also had years of experience in teaching them. Each author had to be known as a gifted instructor who understands the teaching of sport so thoroughly that he or she could readily apply the *steps to success* model.

Next, all of the manuscripts were carefully developed to meet the guidelines of the *steps to success* model. Then our production team, along with outstanding artists, created a highly visual, user-friendly series of books.

The result: The Steps to Success Activity Series is the premier sports instructional series available today.

This series would not have been possible without the contributions of the following:

- Dr. Rainer Martens, publisher,
- Dr. Joan Vickers, instructional design expert,
- the staff of Human Kinetics Publishers, and
- the *many* students, teachers, coaches, consultants, teacher educators, specialists, and administrators who shared their ideas—and dreams.

Judy Patterson Wright
Series Editor

Preface

Most self-defense instruction today comes not from physical educators but from people who have trained, usually for several years, in a martial art such as karate or aikido. The short-term self-defense courses offered by these instructors are often well organized and expertly taught but focus almost exclusively on the development of physical skills. These skills are generally derived from the particular system studied by the instructor and presented in simplified form. Whereas some communities feature a large number of martial arts schools and many affordable options for learning self-defense, others offer very little.

I feel strongly that if knowledge and skills regarding assault prevention and self-defense are to become widely disseminated, they must become a routine part of physical education classes beginning at the latest at the junior-high level. If government statistics about crimes of violence are accurate, then routine presentation of preventive strategies and personal safety skills through the schools is certainly warranted. And who is more competent to present these than physical educators, given their formal training in the teaching of movement skills and their membership in a profession with a long history of involvement in safety-oriented programs, such as water safety instruction and CPR?

Teaching Self-Defense: Steps to Success is primarily intended to be a resource for physical educators with limited background in martial arts or self-defense. It may also be useful to advanced martial artists who are interested in teaching a practical, beginning-level self-defense class but who have limited academic training in designing and teaching physical activities.

In presenting self-defense, this instructor's guide goes beyond the technical skills and drills offered in the participant's book. Ratings charts are included for determining the skill levels of students, and there are suggestions for identifying and correcting common errors. Also offered are a substantial number of modifications of the drills introduced in the participant's book so you can increase or decrease difficulty to match the general ability of your group. Student Options allow you to offer individuals in your classes alternative (and frequently more challenging) drill variations. A substantial appendix features sample lesson plans, individual plans for charting students' progress, and a sample scope and teaching sequence that can serve as a master plan for a semester-long course in self-defense. In addition, there are ideas on how to evaluate students, both with respect to performance of physical skills and to their general knowledge regarding assault prevention. To measure knowledge, I have included a test bank of 68 questions for measuring students' awareness of the nature, circumstances, stages, and psychodynamics of various forms of aggression, and their understanding of the details of preventive strategies, such as de-escalation and assertiveness/confrontation.

Unique about this book and the participant's book is the integrative approach to personal safety. Combined in one comprehensive program are observational, judgment, communication, and physical self-defense skills. Verbal, nonverbal, and psychological techniques enable a defender to postpone physical aggression and defuse potentially volatile situations. Physical self-defense skills are presented as the strategy of last resort—for use when all efforts at prevention of violence fail.

After practicing the preventive skills and strategies introduced in the first three steps, students will focus on mastery of basic physical skills, such as evasions, blocking, and counterattacks. They are then ready to explore the application of these foundation skills to defending against several common attacks, including grab attacks and punching attacks. As your students' technique improves, their practice becomes increasingly improvisational, with ever greater emphasis on perception and judgment. Finally, students participate in drills designed to improve their capacity to stay focused and calm and to think clearly and strategically when faced with the emergency of assault. The importance of learning to resist the panic and confusion that characterize assaultive situations is reflected in the progressively more challenging and realistic drills within each individual step and in the final step, titled Recall Under Stress.

Many people contributed in important ways to the writing of this book, probably none more than the students in my classes who have offered thoughtful and constructive feedback over the years. The very best drills in this book—the most creative and instructive—invariably have come from them. I would also like to thank my "teachers"—people in my life who have provided the information, skills, insight, and inspiration that made possible the writing of this book. They are Robert Parsons, Wayne Wilson, Bobbi Snyder, Barbara Bones, Janesa Kruse, Jaye Spiro, Sunny Graff, and David Nelson.

Thank you, also, to Judy Patterson Wright and Rodd Whelpley of Human Kinetics, for their ex-cellent suggestions and extraordinary patience throughout the writing of both of these books.

And finally, I would like to dedicate this book to my older brother, Mark, for whom so much of the last few years has been, metaphorically speaking, a "bare-knuckled brawl," and to my son, Peter, in hopes that the world in which he grows up is one that requires less and less the acquisition of these skills.

Implementing the Steps to Success Staircase

This book is meant to be flexible not only for your students' needs but for your needs as well. It is common to hear that students' perceptions of a task change as the task is learned. However, it is often forgotten that teachers' perceptions and actions also change (Goc-Karp & Zakrajsek, 1987; Housner & Griffey, 1985; Imwold & Hoffman, 1983; and Vickers, 1990).

More experienced or master teachers tend to approach the teaching of activities in a similar manner. They are highly organized (e.g., they do not waste time getting groups together or using long explanations); they integrate information (from biomechanics, kinesiology, exercise physiology, motor learning, sport psychology, cognitive psychology, instructional design, etc.); and they relate basic skills to the larger game or performance context, succinctly explaining why the basic skills, concepts, and tactics are important to the activity or in the performance setting. Then, usually within a few minutes, they put their students in realistic practice situations that take the students through steps that follow logical manipulations of factors, such as

- possibilities for postponement or avoidance of violence,
- the types of attacks (i.e., grab attacks or punching attacks),
- angles of attack and trajectories of defense,
- the number of skills used in combination,
- the addition or removal of equipment,
- the speed at which skills are performed, and
- the number and intensity of stressors utilized to startle the defender.

This book will show you how the basic self-defense skills and selected physiological, psychological, and other pertinent knowledge are interrelated (see Appendix A for an overview). You can use this information not only to gain insight into the various interrelationships but also to define the subject matter for self-defense. The following questions offer specific suggestions for implementing this knowledge base and help you evaluate and improve your teaching methods, including class organization, drills, objectives, progressions, and evaluations.

1. Under what conditions do you teach?
   - How much space is available?
   - What type of equipment is available?
   - What is the average class size?
   - How much time is allotted to each class session?
   - How many class sessions do you teach?
   - Do you have any teaching assistants?

2. What are your students' initial skill levels?
   - Look for the rating charts located in the beginning of most steps (chapters) to identify the criteria that discriminate between beginning and skilled levels.

3. What is the best order in which to teach self-defense skills?
   - Follow the sequence of steps (chapters) used in this book.
   - See Appendix B.1 for suggestions on when to introduce, review, or continue practicing each step (assuming a 50-minute class session).
   - Based on your answers to the previous questions, use the form in Appendix B.2 to put into order the steps that you will be able to cover in the time available for your classes.

4. What objectives do you want your students to accomplish by the end of a lesson, unit, or couse?
   - For technique or qualitative objectives, select from the Student Keys to Success (or see the Keys to Success Checklists in *Self-Defense: Steps to Success*) that are provided for all basic skills.
   - For performance or quantitative objectives, select from the Student Success Goals provided for each drill.
   - For written questions on safety, rules, technique, history, and psychological aspects of self-defense, select from the Test Bank of written questions.
   - See the Sample Individual Program (in Appendix C.1) for selected technique and performance objectives for a 16-week unit.

- For unit objectives, adjust the total number of selected objectives to fit your unit length (use the form in Appendix C.2).
- For organizing daily objectives, review the Sample Lesson Plan in Appendix D.1 and use the basic lesson plan form in Appendix D.2 to best fit your needs.

5. How will you evaluate your students?

- Read "Evaluation Ideas."
- Decide on a grading system; you could use letter grades, pass-fail, total points, percentages, skill levels (e.g., bronze, silver, gold), and so forth.

6. Which activities should be selected to achieve student objectives?

- Follow the drills for each step; they are specifically designed for large groups and are presented in easy-to-difficult order. Avoid a random approach to selecting drills and exercises.
- Modify drills as necessary to best fit each student's skill level by following the suggestions for decreasing or increasing the difficulty level of each drill.

- Encourage students to meet the Success Goal listed for each drill.
- Use the cross-reference to the corresponding step and drill in the participant's book, *Self-Defense: Steps to Success*, for class assignments or makeups.

7. What rules and expectations do you have for your class?

- For general management and safety guidelines, read "Preparing Your Class for Success."
- For specific guidelines, read the Group Management and Safety Tips included with each drill.
- During class orientation or on the first day of class, tell your students what your rules are. Then post the rules and refer to them often.

Teaching is a complex task, which requires you to make many decisions that affect both you and your students (see Figure 1). Use this book to create an effective and successful learning experience for you and everyone you teach. And remember, have fun, too!

Key*

A = attacker
D = defender
I = instructor
X = students
——▶ = direction of attacker's movement
- - - ▶ = direction of defender's movement

*Note: Because only a small number of the violent crimes committed are reported to authorities, it is impossible to determine precisely the proportions by sex and race of those involved. The "attackers" (A) and "defenders" (D) featured in the illustrations reflect a composite of current government statistics and independent research on perpetrators and victims of violent crime.

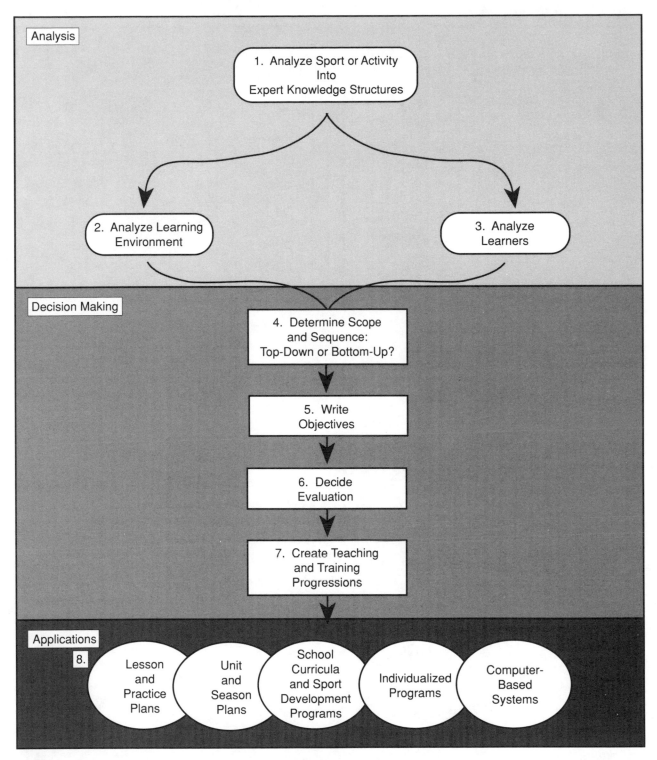

Figure 1   Instructional design model utilizing expert knowledge structures. *Note.* From *Instructional Design for Teaching Physical Activities* by J.N. Vickers, 1990, Champaign, IL: Human Kinetics. Copyright 1990 by Joan N. Vickers. Reprinted by permission. This instructional design model has appeared in earlier forms in *Badminton: A Structures of Knowledge Approach* (p. 1) by J.N. Vickers and D. Brecht, 1987, Calgary, AB: University Printing Services, copyright 1987 by Joan N. Vickers; and in "The Role of Expert Knowledge Structures in an Instructional Design Model for Physical Education" by J.N. Vickers, 1983, *Journal of Teaching in Physical Education*, **2**(3), p. 20, copyright 1983 by Joan N. Vickers.

Preparing Your Class for Success

Before you begin teaching your self-defense classes, you need to think about general procedures and patterns of organization. The following suggestions give you guidance in creating an effective and safe learning environment.

GENERAL CLASS MANAGEMENT

When preparing for and making decisions about the day-to-day operation of your class, consider the following points:

• Over 1/3 of your class sessions are likely to utilize a varied instructional format, including lecture, guided discussion, perhaps some role-playing, and several physical activity drills. Determine in advance how much time you'll need for each of these. Prepare to be both flexible and efficient in managing topics and activities.

• Skill-building activities and drills will generally proceed from simple to complex, half-speed to full-speed, and from exercises done alone to those done with partners.

• Always include group warm-ups and cool-downs when doing physical activity drills.

• Note that, in some steps, drills that are separate and distinct in the participant's book are treated as one, long, multifaceted drill in the instructor's book. Knitting the drills together in this way is intended to promote easy and efficient flow from one drill to the next. The need to set up a new drill that has essentially the same format as the drill that preceded it has been eliminated. Ultimately, this allows for greater time-on-task and a better sense of how the drills fit together to form a fluid whole.

• Continually encourage an attitude of respect and support for practice partners and a concern for everyone's safety. Discourage competitiveness and horseplay during class.

• Keep in mind that a significant number of your students are likely to be survivors of sexual assault, incest, or other forms of violence. Class activities and discussions may trigger flashbacks or bring up painful memories. Acknowledge this during your first meeting, and be ready to give these students a time-out when needed. Know that many survivors choose not to share this information, and, of course, their privacy should be respected. Others will readily share their experiences with you or other students. Be sensitive and supportive of students who you know or suspect are survivors of any form of violence or abuse.

• Emphasize throughout the course that self-defense training is not simply the learning of a few movement techniques but the acquisition of a lifestyle of vigilance and preparedness that leads to greater security and peace of mind than one would otherwise have.

CLASS ORGANIZATION TECHNIQUES

In order to make the most efficient use of time and space, you may wish to consider these suggestions:

• Make sure that the workout space is large enough to allow your students sufficient room to safely practice. Specifically, always be sure that there is at least 4 feet between individuals during solo drills and between pairs during partner drills.

• Provide clear, concise descriptions when demonstrating a skill. Point out how the technique is done and why it is executed in a particular way. Include both biomechanical and strategic explanations when addressing the why of the technique. Be sure to demonstrate the technique with and without a partner, so that students understand the application. Include suggestions about how to practice a skill safely.

• For partner drills, line your students up in two even lines with partners facing one another (as if they were about to do the Virginia reel). This enables you to move quickly and easily down the lines to give feedback to individual students as they practice. Keep your feedback brief and concise in order to maximize students' repetitions (see Figure 2).

• If you see an error being repeated by several students, stop the activity and give group feedback. Have a signal, such as one blast on a whistle, to bring the group back together for

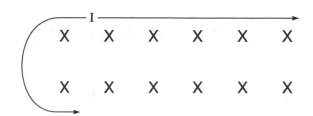

Figure 2 The "Virginia reel" format allows you to move up and down the lines to give feedback to students.

further explanation, demonstration, or group feedback.

• For partner drills, limit the length of time each student plays defender or attacker to no more than 2 minutes. Be sure that each partner gets equal time to practice each skill.

• Discourage horseplay or competitiveness whenever you spot it during practice drills. Encourage students to stay focused and to work harmoniously and cooperatively with their partners in order to maximize learning.

• Watch for signs of panic or excessive anxiety, such as an inability to keep eyes closed during drills in which "loss" of vision is a stressor. A student may need additional encouragement, a more supportive partner, your permission to determine his or her own practice pace and intensity, or even a time-out, in the event that the exercise is triggering flashbacks or frightening memories.

• Encourage partner feedback at the *end* of each drill. This facilitates the development of a "critical eye" and makes students more knowledgeable about technique. It also contributes to an attitude of helpfulness and cooperation—useful and important in a setting where people are practicing skills that are frequently designed to hurt or injure another.

• Rotate partners for each drill. Encourage students to work with a wide variety of people, both men and women. An effective way to do this is simply to have students in one line of partners move "one person to the right" to face a new partner for each drill.

CLASS WARM-UPS AND COOL-DOWNS

A thorough warm-up, consisting of aerobic exercise, stretches, and strength-building exercises, prepares your students' bodies for the powerful trunk rotations and ballistic movement frequently employed in self-defense. A stretching cool-down reduces postpractice muscle soreness and leaves your students' bodies (and minds) in a more relaxed state.

Warm-Up

The suggested warm-up can be divided into three phases. The first phase consists of approximately 3 minutes of mild aerobic activity to increase circulation and raise the temperature of blood and muscles. The second phase focuses on flexibility and consists of a series of stretches done over a period of 3 to 5 minutes. The third phase takes about the same length of time and consists of a sequence of strength-building exercises. Lead your students through the suggested exercises in this three-phase warm-up. A description of how they are performed can be found in *Self-Defense: Steps to Success*, pages 6-10.

Phase 1: Aerobic exercise (3 minutes)
        Options: Jogging in place
                 Jumping jacks
                 Brisk walking

Phase 2: Flexibility exercises (3-5 minutes)
        Trunk rotations
        Side stretches
        Six-count body curl
        Arm circles
        Arm sweeps
        Hamstring stretch
        Five-direction neck stretch

Phase 3: Strength-building exercises
          (3-5 minutes)
        Abdominal curls
        Seated leg lifts
        Push-ups

Cool-Down (5 minutes)

When you have finished all the physical activity drills scheduled for a particular class session, lead your class through a 5-minute stretching cool-down by repeating the seven flexibility exercises from Phase 2 of the warm-up sequence. Remind your students to move slowly and gently, to exhale on the stretch, and to focus on the sensation of stretch, softening where they feel the sensation most intensely. This cool-down should leave your students feeling relaxed and centered.

EQUIPMENT

Most of the drills in this book require little or no equipment. The equipment that is required includes mirrors for use with the various solo drills and hand-held shields or bags for the impact drills in Steps 6, 7, and 8.

Mirrors

Full-size, wall-length mirrors of the sort found in dance studios are excellent for use with the solo drills in Steps 4, 5, 6, and 9. Mirrors enable your students to monitor their own stance and execution and to self-correct obvious biomechanical errors.

Hand-Held Shields and Bags

Bags or hand-held shields are used in the impact drills described in *Self-Defense: Steps to Success* for front-facing (Step 6), rear-directed (Step 7), and side-directed (Step 8) counterattacks. Students' strikes and kicks improve considerably with the use of these training aids (see Figure 3).

The best bags are the commercial varieties available in many sporting goods stores or martial arts supply centers. Although bags come in many sizes and lengths, a reasonable size for your purposes is between 45 and 70 pounds and approximately 3 to 4 feet long. Hand-held shields that measure 35 inches by 20 inches by 3 inches are usually available from the same suppliers.

If you are on a limited budget, have your students make their own impact devices by stuffing heavy duffel bags with rags or sawdust and hanging them from secure wall or ceiling holders. Or wrap duct tape around a thick telephone book from a large, metropolitan area, bore a hole through one end, and hang it by a strong cord or chain from a secure ceiling mount. Or, prop a tumbling mat against a wall and tape Xs on it to indicate precise targets.

When using these impact devices, bear in mind that the purpose is to develop precise targeting and biomechanical proficiency. Each time you use these, explain to students that any device provides helpful (and occasionally painful) feedback on correct hand or foot position, trajectory, and targeting. Using such devices dramatically proves the importance of such things as balance, alignment, and movement from larger to smaller muscle groups in generating maximum force with minimal effort.

It's a good idea to post some—if not all—of the following suggestions near your training aids so that students will derive maximum benefit from their use while minimizing injury:

Rules for Using Impact Devices

- Begin with very light impact. Gradually increase to as much as 3/4 power and speed.
- Work for clear trajectories and precise points of contact. To prevent skinned knuckles and other abrasions, avoid skidding on the surface of the device.

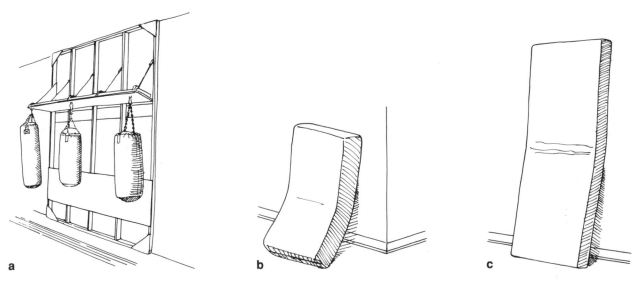

Figure 3 Using impact devices such as (a) a heavy bag, (b) a hand-held shield, or (c) a mat stationed at a wall will help students develop power and accuracy for counterattacks.

- To minimize the risk on impact of jammed fingers, toes, wrists, or ankles, make sure that you use correct hand and foot positions.
- Position yourself in relation to the device as you would be positioned relative to an attacker. Use good defensive stances.
- Do not do impact drills using techniques such as eye gouges and web strikes, which have a high probability of causing jammed fingers.
- Good candidates for impact drills are
  - Front-Facing Counterattacks:
    - Punches
    - Palm-heel strikes
    - Front snap kicks
  - Rear-Directed Counterattacks:
    - Elbow jabs
    - Back kicks
    - Scrapes/Stomps (if you are using a cushioned wall surface)
  - Side-Directed Counterattacks
    - Hammerfist
    - Side stomp kick

Finally, have fun with these. Paint large, red Xs to help your students develop even more precise targeting. Encourage them to whoop and holler and kiyai while executing techniques. Your students will not only improve their technique with these drills, they will feel tremendously empowered by the concrete evidence of their effectiveness at strikes and kicks each time the bag rebounds off the wall.

SAFETY

It seems especially ironic that accidents and injuries can occur in a class about increasing personal safety. Nevertheless, it does happen, and having an established injury and accident procedure is a good idea. There are several steps that you, as an instructor of self-defense, can take to reduce the likelihood of injuries in your classes.

Before Class

- Make sure that the workout space is large enough to accommodate the number of students you have. Students should be able to participate in drills without continually worrying about collisions with others practicing nearby.
- Make sure that floor surfaces are not uneven or slippery.

- Make sure that students with known injuries or impairments have medical approval for participating in your class.

During Class

- Stress safety to your students. When demonstrating technique, emphasize what should be done (or not done) in order to practice the skill safely. Remind students to move more slowly and carefully when they are first learning a technique, and to never exceed about 3/4 maximum power and speed, even when practicing familiar skills.
- Discourage horseplay, competitiveness, and other risky behavior during partner work.
- Know which drills present the greatest risk of injury during practice, and be particularly vigilant when your students are doing them (e.g., impact drills, milling exercises, any partner drill involving use of strikes or kicks).
- Require of your students that they not chew gum or wear jewelry and that they keep fingernails short and wear nonrestrictive clothing and tennis shoes.
- Instruct students to let you know immediately of any injuries to themselves or classmates.

PRECLASS CHECKLIST

Careful planning and preparation of the workout space will help to maximize practice time. Here are some suggestions of things to do *before* your students arrive:

- Have impact devices in place.
- Make sure the floor is cleared of dust and debris and is generally safe for self-defense practice.
- Hang posters and set up flip charts that you intend to use.
- Have a detailed lesson plan. Also have a contingency plan or two, in the event that the first is too simple, too difficult, or finished in less time than expected.

NINE LEGAL DUTIES

As a teacher, you are responsible for providing students with a safe learning environment. In meeting this responsibility, you'll want to attend to the specific safety concerns addressed earlier in this section (see "Equipment" and "Safety"). Also, be familiar with the following legal duties that are required of you as coach/instructor by the judicial system.

1. Adequate Supervision

Do not leave the workout space during class, even for a few moments. During drills, position yourself in a location from which you can effectively monitor all students and activities. Be on the alert for behaviors that frequently lead to injury—competitiveness, horseplay, extreme anxiety, and lack of focus.

2. Sound Planning

As you develop your class plan, consider carefully your students' physical capabilities and skills. Also consider their emotional readiness for certain more challenging exercises and activities. Be sure that your drills progress from simple to more complex—build each defense step-by-reasonable-step.

3. Inherent Risks

Let your students know that there is an inherent risk in the practice of self-defense skills. Consider having them sign a waiver indicating that they understand this fact and willingly undertake the risk. In addition to a general statement regarding risk, point out the safety concerns specific to each technique during your initial demonstration, and repeat them several times during practice.

4. Safe Environment

A safe environment is one that allows plenty of space for vigorous practice of these skills, features a floor that is even and cleared of dust and debris, and is well lit and ventilated. Periodically check impact devices and tighten attachments to ceiling or wall mounts.

5. Evaluating Students' Fitness for the Activity

Generally speaking, the activities and drills in this book can be done safely by high school- or college-age students, across a fairly broad range of fitness levels. However, you must evaluate each student for injuries, limitations, health challenges, or incapacities that may increase their likelihood of incurring injury. You might also look at personal experience in determining ap-propriateness for participation in this class. For instance, a very recent victim of violence may have a particularly hard time with activities that are sure to recall that trauma. Such students may benefit from waiting until they have a bit more emotional distance from the event before taking self-defense.

6. Matching or Equating Students

Most of the drills in this book allow students of varying sizes and levels of skill to work well together. Temperament can be an issue, however. Try to match students who will challenge one another to do their best in a supportive, noncompetitive manner.

7. Emergency First Aid Procedures

You must know and follow the emergency medical procedures required by your school or institution. Be prepared to provide proper first aid in the event of accident or injury.

8. Specific Legal Concerns

In all circumstances, you must respect the civil rights of your students.

9. General Legal Concerns

Despite even strenuous efforts to prevent injuries or accidents, they can still occur, and it is possible that one of these may lead to litigation. For your own legal protection, it is important to keep accurate and detailed records of all incidents that occur in your classes. Also, find out what kind of liability insurance is carried by your institution. Consider carrying additional personal liability insurance for further protection.

Self-defense instructors have been sued for providing inadequate instruction or misinformation to students who subsequently were unsuccessful in defending against an actual assailant. Make sure that the statistical data you give students is accurate and current. Emphasize throughout this class that there are *no* magic formulas or guaranteed outcomes in assaultive situations. Avoid the use of the words *always* and *never*. Reiterate that what is most important in any assault is that the defender have the wherewithal to accurately assess the situation and determine an appropriate (i.e., reasonable, necessary, and effective) response.

Step 1   Awareness

The "Three A's" of personal safety is a mechanism for recalling information and skills useful for protecting oneself in threatening or assaultive circumstances. The three are

- awareness,
- assessment, and
- action.

In your first meeting with students, you'll thoroughly discuss awareness and assessment and provide an overview of the four action strategies in order to give students a clear theoretical framework for the verbal, psychological, and physical skills that they will be learning. This framework is diagrammatically represented in the Continuum of Response (see Figure 1.1).

In your initial presentation of the Three A's, a combination of lecture and guided discussion lets you get out a lot of information while at the same time encouraging students to share ideas and perceptions. By the end of this lecture/discussion, your students should have

- a clear grasp of the nature and circumstances of various forms of assault as reflected in research;
- a knowledge of precautionary measures that tend to reduce vulnerability;
- an appreciation for the importance of quick, accurate assessments of specific situational factors in determining appropriate preventive action; and

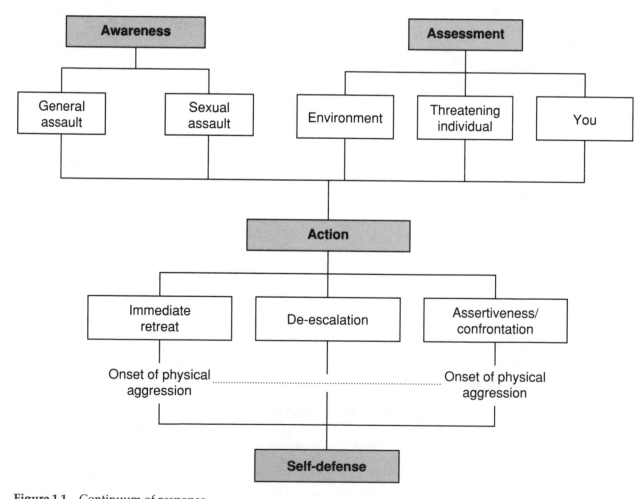

Figure 1.1   Continuum of response.

- a general understanding of the courses of action available in dealing with a potential assailant and the point at which these strategies are useful and appropriate.

A thorough discussion of all the information in Step 1 of *Self-Defense: Steps to Success* will insure that this is accomplished. To get a sense of the flow of information for your introductory lecture, refer to the following outline on this page.

AWARENESS

A thoroughgoing awareness of the nature, typical circumstances, and dynamics of various forms of assaultive behavior is at the heart of assault prevention (see Figure 1.2). The more knowledgeable your students, the more likely they are to be able to *avoid* dangerous situations.

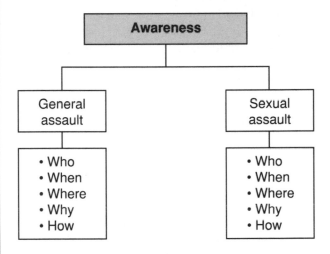

Figure 1.2 Awareness.

Knowledge of this sort can come from many sources, both formal and informal. More formal sources include governmental agencies and private researchers; the data they generate reveal when, where, and with whom we are most at risk. This data also suggests which responses have been most effective in preventing assault.

The participants' book attempts to familiarize your students with information about two broad categories of violent crime—assault and sexual assault. Assault is the more general category, encompassing all manner of aggressive behavior directed toward either females or males in a wide variety of circumstances. Sexual assault refers to that particular form of violence where power, anger, and sexuality meet. This form of

aggression is more often, though not exclusively, directed at females.

Be sure to address both categories in detail (see *Self-Defense*, Step 1, pp. 11-15) and in the order outlined here during your opening lecture:

I. Assault
   A. Frequency of occurrence
      - 5 out of 6 North Americans will be victims (attempted or completed) at least once
   B. Location and time of assault
      - Over half at night
      - In vicinity of victim's home
   C. Victims of assault
      - Family violence: 19% female children, 9% male children, 25% women
      - Outside-of-family violence: young males, minorities, service workers
   D. Typical assailants
      - Family violence: 90% are males from all backgrounds
      - Outside-of-family violence: 18 to 34 years old, male, white, known, altered by drugs or alcohol

II. Sexual assault
   A. Frequency of occurrence
      - 1 in 5 women
      - 1 in 10 men
   B. Victims of sexual assault
      - All backgrounds and ages
      - Appear to assailants to be vulnerable and accessible
      - Victims do *not* dress or act provocatively
      - Underreported and rarely falsely reported
   C. Sexual assailants
      - Come from all backgrounds
      - Known to victim more than half the time
      - Most assaults are planned
      - Intraracial as opposed to interracial
      - Motivated by power, anger, or sadism
   D. Stages of sexual assault
      - 1. Selection
      - 2. Testing
      - 3. Force
   E. The question of resistance
      - Always your personal decision
      - Studies suggest immediate and vigorous resistance will usually deter unarmed assailant

Awareness Drills

Both Awareness Drills are intended to be done outside of self-defense class, either as homework or for additional credit. The two drills, "Self-Study of Precautionary Measures" and "Special Projects," can be assigned during the first and second weeks of class, respectively. (Suggestions for weekly out-of-class assignments are included in Appendix B.1, How to Use the Scope and Teaching Sequence Form.)

Be sure to allow time in subsequent classes for students to share their work with one another and with you.

1. Self-Study of Precautionary Measures
[Corresponds to *Self-Defense*, Step 1, Drill 1]

Group Management Tips

- Gather students together to discuss this assignment and the self-study forms in their books.
- Emphasize that this is intended to help each of them identify areas in their lives where they can reduce vulnerability and accessibility to an assailant.
- Point out that students will not be graded on this self-study, that it is solely for their own information.
- Ask students to complete this study before a designated class meeting, at which time students will have the option of sharing and discussing results.

Instructions to Class

- "Conduct a self-study to determine areas of your life where you can reduce your vulnerability and accessibility to an assailant. Use the Self-Study Precautions form found on pages 15-17 of *Self-Defense: Steps to Success* to look specifically at the lists of precautions you might take (a) in the street, (b) in your home, and (c) in your car. Assign a point value to each precaution, and then total your points. If you fall short of 80% of the maximum possible, consider incorporating more of these preventive behaviors into your daily routines. Keep in mind that your goal is not to limit your options or circumscribe behavior, but rather to blend into your life those practices that will enable you to live your life with a greater sense of security."

Student Option

- Suggest several different situations in which one might feel at risk, and then brainstorm with your students about possible precautionary measures that might be taken in order to reduce one's vulnerability and accessibility under these circumstances. For example, the following are a few such situations (and some precautionary measures):

Situation 1
You are working late in a high-crime neighborhood. Your car is parked in a dark lot some distance from your building.

Precautionary Measures
1. Move your car closer to the building earlier in the evening when spaces open up and before it is dark.
2. Arrange to work late when someone else is doing the same. Walk to your cars together, or arrange to share a ride.

Situation 2
You are traveling alone and are staying in a hotel in a high-crime area of a city with which you are unfamiliar.

Precautionary Measures

1. Consider moving to a hotel where you will feel safer.
2. Ask ahead of time (for instance, while making reservations) about measures the hotel has taken to insure the safety of guests.
3. Ask for a second-story or higher room. (Avoid the ground floor.)
4. Make sure doors have dead bolts and windows are equipped with strong locks.
5. Ask to be put on a floor where there are a number of other guests.
6. Take a tour after you check in and note avenues of escape, hall lighting, etc.

Situation 3

You are camping alone in a state campground in order to do some solo day hikes on a nearby system of trails.

Precautionary Measures

1. Cruise through the campground when you first arrive. Select a campsite near a family or a retired couple. (*Author's note*: My personal experience is that these folks are the most likely to befriend and watch out for you.)
2. Let your newfound friends or a park ranger know which trail you'll be hiking on a particular day and the time you expect to return to the campground.

3. Consider investing in a camper or van that can be locked at night. Or use a miniature lock to secure your tent zipper(s).
4. At night, place a large duffel directly in front of and inside the entrance of your tent.
5. Keep a shriek alarm or a whistle under your pillow to alert others if someone tries to enter your tent at night. (Be sure you can distinguish between human intruders and a raccoon raiding your campsite for food.)

Student Success Goals

- In the street (80% of maximum possible or 9 points)
- In your home (80% of maximum possible or 10 points)
- In your car (80% of maximum possible or 6 points)
- Total points for precautionary measures (80% or 25 points)

To Reduce Difficulty

- N/A

To Increase Difficulty

- N/A

2. *Special Projects*
[Corresponds to *Self-Defense*, Step 1, Drill 2]

Group Management Tips

- Gather students together to discuss this project. Point out that each of the four exercises is intended to increase awareness of the social context in which violence and aggression occur. Discuss all four options found on pages 17 and 18 of the participant's book, and answer any questions that may arise.
- Ask students to select one of the four and to be prepared to report back to the group on their findings on a designated date. Explain that these oral reports should be no longer than 2 minutes in length and that

students also should turn in a one-page typewritten report on their findings. Explain that though no specific grade will be given for the report, each student is expected to complete one. Point out that completion of a project will be noted and considered in determining each student's final grade for the course.
- Set aside the last half of the class period during the fifth class meeting for each student to take a couple of minutes to report and briefly discuss results (see the Sample Scope and Teaching Sequence in Appendix B.1). These exercises can be quite thought provoking, and students' reports can engender

some lively discussions, which may continue outside of class.

- Remember that your goal is to increase your students' understanding of the complexity of the problem of interpersonal violence while encouraging consideration and discussion of possible solutions. Frame your own questions and comments during the presentation and discussions in such a way that your group stays focused on the social context in which violence arises and on the societal strategies and measures that may prove effective in reducing violence.

Instructions and Cues to Class

- "From the projects suggested on pages 17 and 18, select one that you have time for and interest in doing. Be prepared to make a brief, 2-minute oral presentation of your findings and insights to the group. Also, discuss your findings in a written report of approximately one typewritten page in length, and turn it in on the day you make your oral report."

Student Options

- "Come up with an alternative project more to your liking, but still related to the social context of violence and requiring about the same investment of time and energy (approximately 2 hours) as the four provided."

Student Success Goal

- Deliver oral report and typewritten report

To Reduce Difficulty

- N/A

To Increase Difficulty

- N/A

Step 2 Assessment

As with Awareness, a lecture or guided discussion is an appropriate format for introducing Assessment, the process of quickly and accurately evaluating a specific situation in which one feels at risk.

Begin by stressing the importance of presence of mind and solid observational and perceptual skills in assessing a potentially dangerous situation. Then discuss how to assess a situation using the outline presented in Figure 2.1 and noting those details regarding

- the immediate environment,
- the threatening individual, and
- the threatened individual.

Take these one at a time, beginning with the immediate environment. Have your students generate a list of what might be important about the environment in which an attack is threatened. If your students are slow to offer ideas, ask them to imagine themselves in potentially assaultive environments, such as parking garages, parking lots, city streets, hotel corridors, office buildings, or one's own living room. Guide them toward recognition of the importance of noting avenues of escape, shields, barriers, and other people.

When generating the list of things to note about the threatening individual, jog your students' imaginations by providing examples of hypothetical aggressors, for example, an intrusive stranger at a bus stop, the coworker who does not respect personal space and asks personal questions, the date who ignores limits and boundaries that one attempts to impose, or the emotionally unstable client or customer with whom one has contact. Ask students to focus on *behavioral* cues that reveal an agitated or aggressive state of mind and violent intentions.

When discussing the third part of assessment—the threatened individual—invite students to think about the strengths, skills, and

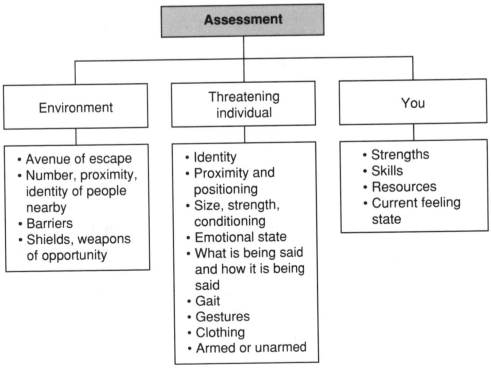

Figure 2.1 Assessment.

resources that serve one in *any* emergency, such as presence of mind, physical courage, physical strength, and speed.

At the completion of this approximately 15-minute discussion, your students should know what minimal factors about the environment, the threatening individual, and themselves to consider in any potentially dangerous situation.

Make sure that the three lists generated by your group include all of those factors outlined in *Self-Defense*, Step 2, pp. 19-20, and perhaps more.

When you have thoroughly discussed Assessment, assign the following drills. Again, these can be assigned as out-of-class projects (see the schedule included in Appendix B.1).

Assessment Drills

1. *Environment Assessment Drill*
[Corresponds to *Self-Defense*, Step 2, Drill 1]

Group Management Tips

- Gather your students and explain that the purpose of this drill is to increase skill in rapidly processing information about the setting in which an assault is threatened.
- Indicate the date by which the drill should be completed.

Instructions and Cues to Class

- "Conduct a tour of 10 different sites within close proximity of one another. Be sure to include several rooms in your home, as well as other indoor sites where you spend significant time, for example, your office or work environment, hallways, or classrooms. Also include a number of outdoor sites, such as your driveway, parking garages that you use, or routes that you typically walk."
- "Once positioned at each site, give yourself 10 seconds to take in as much information about the setting as possible. Minimally, this should include those four factors that influence how you might respond to a threatened attack in each particular area, that is (a) avenues of escape, (b) presence of barriers, (c) availability of shields and weapons of opportunity, and (d) proximity and location of other people."

Student Options

- "Consider how assessing any of your sites at a different time of day changes things. For example, are there more or fewer people around? Is lighting better or poorer?"

- "Get into the habit of routinely assessing new environments in terms of safety. For the duration of the class, give yourself the goal of conducting a quick assessment of a different site each day. You need not spend a lot of time on this. As you walk into a classroom, stroll through a slightly unfamiliar neighborhood, enter an office building, or visit a friend's home, quietly and quickly take note of avenues of escape, shields and barriers, the presence of others, and so on. The process becomes increasingly automatic over time, until you may find yourself routinely doing this in any new environment. This habit may be especially useful if your profession often places you at some risk, for example, law enforcement, some human service occupations, or traveling sales.

Student Success Goal

- Visit 10 sites and assess key elements of the environment at each site in 10 seconds or less

To Decrease Difficulty

- Allow more time to process information about the setting (e.g., 30 seconds).

To Increase Difficulty

- Reduce the time allowed to process information about a setting to 5 seconds.

2. People-Reading Drill

[Corresponds to *Self-Defense*, Step 2, Drill 2]

Group Management Tips

- Gather your students and explain that the purpose of this drill is to help them to become more aware of the behavioral cues that suggest particular emotional states in others and, in particular, those emotional states associated with violence and aggression. Review those factors discussed earlier, such as identity of threatening individual, positioning and proximity to threatened person, size, appearance of strength, demeanor, stance, posture, gestures, coloring (flushed, pale), gait, clothes, and pitch, tone, and volume of voice (see *Self-Defense*, Step 2, pp. 19-20 for detailed descriptions of these factors, particularly as they relate to highly agitated individuals).

- Discuss possible methods and locations for people-reading, such as boxing matches, airports, football games, in films or television shows, and plays.
- Assign a date by which this assignment should be completed. Ask students to be prepared to discuss their observations with the group at that time. (See Appendix B.1.)

Student Success Goals

- 30 minutes of people-reading
- Discuss observations with group at designated time

To Reduce Difficulty

- N/A

To Increase Difficulty

- N/A

3. Self-Assessment Drill

[Corresponds to *Self-Defense*, Step 2, Drill 3]

Group Management Tips

- Gather your group and explain that the purpose of this drill is to help them clarify and affirm the skills, strengths, and personal resources that they bring to potentially assaultive situations using the Inventory of Skills/Strengths (see *Self-Defense*, Step 2, pp. 21-22). Students generally *underestimate* their own strengths, so encourage them to examine the impact of indirectly related experiences and skills (e.g., the strength, endurance, agility, and balance derived from involvement in sports or dance; a self-confident and erect posture; being slow to panic; general attentiveness and awareness of surroundings; a capacity for quick thinking or problem-solving).
- Suggest that as they do the inventory students try to recall their responses to other sorts of emergencies and to think about how these capacities might be used to best advantage in preventing assault.

- Invite students to identify five or more areas of possible improvement.
- Indicate the date by which the Inventory of Skills/Strengths is to be completed (see Sample Scope and Teaching Sequence in Appendix B.1).

Instructions and Cues to Class

- "Carefully complete the Inventory of Skills/Strengths by rating each item on a scale of 1 to 5, with 1 indicating *none or little* and 5 indicating *a great deal* of that particular strength, skill, or capacity. Circle the number that most closely reflects your ability."
- "When you've completed the inventory, identify those areas in which you would most like to improve and think about how you might do so. List those areas."

Student Option

- "Repeat this inventory at the end of this course and note the changes."

Student Success Goals

- Completion of Inventory of Skills/Strengths
- Identification of 5 areas of potential improvement

To Reduce Difficulty

- N/A

To Increase Difficulty

- N/A

Step 3   Action

The action we take in a potentially assaultive situation is based on the interplay between our general knowledge and experience of interpersonal aggression (Awareness) and our rapid evaluation of an immediately threatening situation (Assessment). Action is also based on an understanding of strategies for defense and their possible outcomes.

The four Action strategies presented in this book are Immediate Retreat, De-Escalation, Assertiveness/Confrontation, and Self-Defense. The first three strategies involve actions taken *before* the onset of physical aggression—before the student is struck, pushed, or grabbed. The fourth, Self-Defense, refers to tactics used in response to an actual physical attack and is, whenever possible, the strategy of last resort. By the time they complete this course, your students should be able to select and implement the action strategy most appropriate to a variety of threatening circumstances.

SOME SUGGESTIONS FOR YOUR FIRST CLASS PERIOD

In the Sample Scope and Teaching Sequence in Appendix B.1, you'll notice that in the first class period a theoretical overview of the course is planned, but time for the practice of self-defense skills is also allowed. By the time your students leave this class, they should understand the range of skills to be covered and have already begun to work on new movement skills.

Assuming you have already spent time during this class on Awareness and Assessment, briefly outline for your students the four Action Strategies they will be practicing and, in time, mastering. Refer to Figure 3.1 to underscore the importance of using the first three strategies—Immediate Retreat, De-Escalation, and Assertiveness/Confrontation—in order to avoid having to use the fourth, Self-Defense.

After this brief naming of the four Action strategies, begin a more in-depth treatment of Immediate Retreat. This should take no more than 5 minutes. Then proceed to a very limited discussion of De-Escalation and Assertiveness/Confrontation. To cover either of these strategies in depth requires two or three entire class periods. Rather than spend the time to do this now, limit yourself to a brief 1-minute description of each. (Reassure your students that they will have the opportunity to work on these strategies in depth midway through the course.)

This brief description might involve simply pointing out that these two strategies consist of

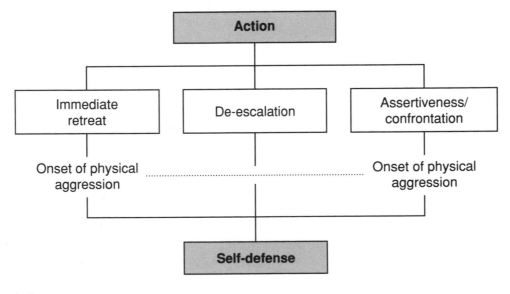

Figure 3.1   Action.

verbal, psychological, and nonverbal techniques for postponing physical aggression in two very different contexts. De-escalation techniques enable a defender to build a sense of connectedness and rapport with a highly agitated individual in order to defuse a rapidly escalating situation. The potential attacker in these situations is generally someone who is extremely angry, frustrated, fearful, intoxicated, or, perhaps, suffering from a brain or spinal malfunction. Explain that, in contrast, assertiveness/confrontation skills are useful when dealing with someone who is attempting to establish a process of dominance. A typical circumstance is during the testing stage of sexual assault.

Finally, point out that in an actual assaultive situation, these "soft" skills would be applied *before* the physical self-defense skills that students will be learning.

Last, introduce Self-Defense, the fourth Action strategy. This will lead you into the practice of the first self-defense technique, described in Step 4.

You can see that this makes for a fairly jam-packed initial class meeting. By the end of this session, you will have thoroughly discussed Awareness and Assessment, and, of the Action strategies, covered Immediate Retreat, briefly defined De-Escalation and Assertiveness/Confrontation, and begun Self-Defense. And you will have met your goal of providing a theoretical context for the practice of these skills and gotten your students moving during the first class meeting.

THE FOUR ACTION STRATEGIES

The coverage of action strategies should proceed little by little throughout the course as noted in the Sample Scope and Teaching Sequence in Appendix B.1.

Immediate Retreat

It should be obvious to your students that immediate retreat provides the best possible chance of avoiding injury or harm in most potentially assaultive situations. Some of your students may feel that retreating in some circumstances (e.g., when confronted by an intoxicated bully at a party) would result in losing face or being perceived as a coward. When discussing the option of walking away from this sort of situation, point out that most states have laws *requiring* retreat from potential violence whenever possible.

Discuss with your students various sets of circumstances that they feel would warrant immediate retreat. Point out that these preemptive escapes from potentially dangerous situations involve moving toward safety *as quickly as circumstances warrant*. To illustrate how one's perception of the imminence of attack determines the *manner* in which one retreats (i.e., how noisily and quickly), include the two examples offered in *Self-Defense*, Step 3, p. 23.

De-Escalation

As suggested previously, provide only a one- or two-sentence description of this strategy during your opening class, and note where it falls on the Continuum of Response. Return to this section at midcourse for detailed guidance on teaching de-escalation skills. Keep in mind that at that time, you'll be devoting one or more entire class periods to skill-building in this area alone.

During your midcourse presentation of de-escalation to your students, explain that this form of "soft self-defense" consists of verbal, psychological, and nonverbal techniques for defusing a potentially explosive situation. Point out that the goal of de-escalation is to build rapid rapport and a sense of connectedness with an agitated person in order to reduce the likelihood of physical violence. Emphasize that de-escalation involves being able to control one's own emotional response and communication in order to reverse the dynamics of a situation that is spiraling out of control.

Discuss the context in which these skills may be useful. Point out that they are generally helpful in dealing with people who are highly agitated, frustrated, angry, fearful, or intoxicated. Indeed, de-escalation skills are often used by people whose jobs bring them into contact with volatile or disruptive individuals. Examples include social workers confronted by irate clients, bartenders trying to "cut off" intoxicated customers, law enforcement personnel trying to talk with an abusive spouse during a domestic call, retail workers assisting frazzled and short-tempered customers, public health investigators threatened by frightened, angry, and potentially disease-carrying citizens, or mental health professionals dealing with out-of-control patients and clients. **Note that de-escalation skills are not appropriate for use with potential sexual assailants, given the distinct psychodynamics**

of sexual aggression. (See "Assertiveness/Confrontation Skills," pp. 22-23.)

Finally, focus on how to de-escalate. List and thoroughly discuss each of the three nonverbal and the six verbal principles of de-escalation as presented in *Self-Defense*, Step 3, pp. 24-27 and outlined in Figure 3.2. Throughout the discussion, ask your students to examine their own experiences for the successful (or unsuccessful) application of these principles. By the end of this approximately 50-minute lecture/discussion, students should have a clear grasp of behaviors that should be avoided (escalating behaviors) and those that may be helpful (defusing techniques).

When you have completed the lecture/discussion on De-Escalation, allow another 50 minutes of class time for De-Escalation Drills 1 and 3 (corresponding to *Self-Defense*, Step 3, Drills 1 & 3) and assign De-Escalation Drill 2 (corresponding to *Self-Defense*, Step 3, Drill 2) for homework.

Note: To learn more about this relatively new area in self-defense training, read the books by Bolton, Haldane, Henley, and Pease listed under "Suggested Readings" in *Self-Defense: Steps to Success*, p. 147. Additional sources for new information and research on dealing with conflict, crisis, or violence include various professional journals in communications, psychology, and criminal justice. If you don't subscribe to many of these, ask colleagues and friends in these disciplines to pass along pertinent articles. Remember that the principles presented here are eclectic and are culled from fairly diverse sources.

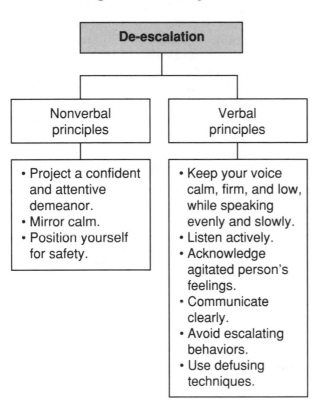

Figure 3.2 De-escalation.

De-Escalation Drills

1. *Nonverbal Principles Practice Drill*
[Corresponds to *Self-Defense*, Step 3, De-Escalation Drill 1]

Group Management Tips

- Divide your group into teams of three. Ask one member of each team to be a monitor and to stand a few feet away from the other two. Have the remaining two students stand facing one another.
- If, after forming your teams of three, you are left with one or two students, add each extra person to one of the other three-person teams to make four-person teams. Larger teams will have two, rather than one, observers.
- Explain that the purpose of the drill is to sharpen students' awareness of their own nonverbal behaviors in a threatening situation. Tell students that you'll be presenting a situation, "The Parking Lot Scene," and

that both of the two students facing one another should imagine that they are characters in the situation.

- Be sure that observers understand that during this first drill, only the top portion, "Nonverbal Principles," will be used.

- When the pair have been scored, students switch roles so that the student(s) who formerly observed may practice the skills and get feedback.

Instructions and Cues to Class

- Read "Parking Lot Scene" to set up the situation.

Parking Lot Scene

You have a temporary job directing traffic in a makeshift parking lot set up to accommodate the large number of spectators attending a major sporting event on your campus. Given the makeshift nature of the lot, parking lanes and spaces are not clearly marked. To complicate things, there are large crowds of people on foot who have already parked their cars and are walking toward the stadium. The game has just begun and those people still having to park are eager to do so. You approach a vehicle to direct the driver to a space he's unable to see clearly. Before you say anything, the man at the wheel begins to complain loudly and angrily about the wait. He berates the lack of adequate parking facilities and what he considers incompetent help. The other passengers are amused by the driver's anger and goad him on. Both driver and passengers appear to have been drinking. You interrupt to direct the driver to the available parking space, not realizing that another attendant has just directed another car to the same spot. The angles of approach of the two vehicles are such that the drivers don't see one another until they collide. Both drivers jump out of their vehicles and are angrily shouting at each other as you dash up to them. The driver with whom you've just been talking suddenly turns on you, shouting and waving his arms threateningly.

- "Imagine that the person you are facing is this highly agitated, potentially explosive driver. In the next few seconds, incorporate as many of the suggestions as you can remember regarding nonverbal principles of de-escalation."

- "Observer(s), note the nonverbal behaviors of the two people facing one another. For each behavior you observe, mark a '1' on the feedback form next to those behaviors we have identified as useful in defusing a situation. Count up the total."

Equipment

- Sufficient copies of the De-Escalation Feedback Form on hand to distribute 3 or 4 to each group (observer[s] will complete 1 for each person practicing the nonverbal skills)

Student Options

- N/A

Student Success Goal

- 7 out of 10 possible points for correctly demonstrating nonverbal behaviors involved in de-escalation

To Decrease Difficulty

- N/A

To Increase Difficulty

- N/A

De-Escalation Feedback Form

Nonverbal Behaviors *(Gain 1 point each)*

Assume a confident and vigilant demeanor.

____ Eyes on other person's eyes?

____ Facial expression neutral?

____ Posture relaxed and alert?

____ Movement/gestures minimized?

Mirror calm.

____ Breathing deeply and slowly?

____ Using positive self-talk (as self-reported)?

Position yourself for safety.

____ Distance of 2 arms'-lengths?

____ Body angled at 45 degrees?

____ Hands free and in front of body?

____ Using available barriers?

Verbal Behaviors *(Gain 1 point each)*

____ Using calm, controlled voice?

____ Active listening?

____ Acknowledging feelings?

____ Clear communication?

____ Use of defusing techniques:

    ____ Brainstorming solutions?

    ____ Redirecting?

    ____ Person sitting down?

    ____ Changing immediate environment?

    ____ Getting to Yes agreement?

    ____ Using humor effectively?

    ____ Defining behavioral limits?

Escalating Behaviors *(Lose 1 point each)*

____ Not listening to or ignoring the person?

____ Threatening?

____ Making unkind or hurtful remarks?

____ Arguing?

____ Commanding?

____ Shouting?

____ Invading space?

____ Using threatening gestures?

____ Using obscenities?

____ Competing?

____ Sounding self-righteous?

Your Score = ____ nonverbal points + ____ verbal points – ____ escalating behaviors = ____ total points

Other observations _____

Primary strengths _____

Suggestions for improvement _____

2. Self-Monitoring Drill

[Corresponds to *Self-Defense*, Step 3, De-Escalation Drill 2]

Group Management Tips

- Gather your students and again discuss the impact on a threatening and agitated individual of maintaining control over one's own fears and anxieties. Emphasize that feeling and projecting calm under these circumstances is something we can learn to do better.
- Explain that this drill is designed to increase each student's ability to maintain a calm and centered presence in stressful circumstances. Students first will determine their general emotional patterns and then consciously experiment with techniques for improvement.

Instructions and Cues to Class

- "Over the next 2 weeks, pay attention to how you generally respond to stressful or even threatening incidents. Be especially conscious of changes in your breathing patterns (Do you hold your breath? Take shallow breaths? Breathe more rapidly?) and self-talk (Is what you are saying to yourself affirming or undermining?)."

- "When you've identified some general patterns, consciously try to slow and deepen your breathing in response to similar incidents as they arise. Also, come up with some simple, confidence-bolstering statements to use in these situations, such as 'I can handle this.'"
- "At the end of the 2 weeks, list the three most stressful situations you encountered, your immediate self-talk, and possible affirmations you might have used (or, in fact, did use)."

Student Options

- N/A

Student Success Goal

- Completion of drill as assigned

To Decrease Difficulty

- N/A

To Increase Difficulty

- N/A

3. Role-Playing/The Lost Project Report

[Corresponds to *Self-Defense*, Step 3, De-Escalation Drill 3]

Group Management Tips

- Divide the group into teams of three. Explain that for this role-playing exercise, one person on each team will play a highly agitated individual, another will attempt to de-escalate the first, and the third will be an observer whose task will be to watch the interaction over a 60-second period and then give feedback.
- Explain that each role play will be limited to 1 minute and that during this time students should remain "in character." In addition, remind the person playing the agitated individual to respond realistically to the de-escalator's efforts by calming down or becoming more upset, depending on whether she or he finds the de-escalator's behaviors calming or inflammatory.

- Instruct observers to stand a few feet away, in order not to interfere with the interaction or to be obtrusive in any way but still close enough to be able to hear what their teammates say. Remind them to note both nonverbal and verbal behaviors on the feedback form, so that they can report accurately to teammates on their "conversational dance."
- When roles are assigned, give a loud verbal cue ("Begin!") to signal a start to the 1-minute role play. At the end of 1 minute, shout "Stop!" Unless you start and stop the role play, students unfamiliar with this format will often cut it short and limit the likelihood of their staying "in character" long enough to get comfortable with role-playing as a learning tool.

- When the role play is completed, ask the three team members to take a few minutes to discuss the interaction (and to decompress!). Instruct the observers to share their observations with teammates at this time regarding the application of nonverbal and verbal de-escalation techniques. Remind observers to note what was done particularly well by the de-escalator, as well as what might be improved.
- Repeat the role play twice more, so that each team member has an opportunity to play all three roles. After each role play, allow a few minutes for team members to discuss among themselves the dynamics of the interaction. This discussion not only clarifies and highlights important aspects of the interaction, but also provides "down time" between what are sometimes fairly intense and challenging role plays. Even though these are not "real" situations, the emotions experienced by participants are real enough to require a breather and the opportunity to process with teammates what was going on for them.
- When all role-playing has been completed, call your students back together to share their observations and insights. These role plays have a way of surprising folks—demonstrating in some an unexpected capacity for calm, clear reasoning under duress and in others, a tongue-tied confusion and paralysis in the face of verbal threat. Encourage students to note and affirm their strengths and to identify for themselves areas to work on (e.g., awareness of range, eye contact, voice quality, offering a listening presence).
- Some of your students may balk at participating in role plays and prefer to simply watch. While watching others role play is interesting and even instructive, it will not provide an opportunity for sharpening and honing these "soft self-defense skills" in the way that being involved in a simulation will. Emphasize that these skills, just like physical self-defense skills, improve with practice. And what people *practice* is generally what they *do* in an actual assault situation, where the stresses are far greater than those associated with role-playing.
- By initially taking a highly structured approach to this exercise and providing a very detailed role play, you can reduce some of the stress and discomfort many people associate with role-playing. After your students have done a few role plays and are more comfortable with this format, loosen up and allow creative deviations from situations you ask them to act out.

Equipment

- Sufficient copies of the De-Escalation Feedback Form on hand to distribute 3 or 4 to each group

Instructions and Cues to Class

- "This role-playing drill provides an opportunity to practice de-escalation skills in a simulated situation that I will describe shortly. One member of each team will play an 'agitated person' and one will play a 'de-escalator.' Remain 'in character' for 1 minute. During this 1-minute simulation, the observer will note on the feedback form all of those listed verbal and nonverbal behaviors incorporated by the de-escalator. Then after the role play, the observer will share his or her observations regarding posture, stance, positioning, demeanor, quality of the voice, and use of either escalating or defusing techniques. During this discussion and processing time, role players will also analyze the dynamics of the interaction, noting when they felt the tension lessening or increasing and discussing possible reasons for this."
- "Here is the role-play situation:

Lost Project Report

The agitated person has come into an office shared with the de-escalator. The former begins to look for a project report left on a worktable the night before. This project is to be turned in to a supervisor within half an hour. Failure to do so may result in severe sanctions for the agitated person, who already has been placed on probationary status for failure to complete work assignments in a timely manner.

The worktable is a mess, due in large part to the de-escalator's sloppy work habits. The project report—finished only the night before and after considerable effort—can't be found. The agitated person has a number of other problems in his or her life at the moment. These other problems (severe and complicated family problems, illness, other deadlines) have created an extraordinary level of stress.

The agitated person becomes increasingly angry, frustrated, and distraught at not being able to find the project report. You, the sloppy office mate, walk in to face this person."

- "Now, begin the role play!"

Student Option

- "Now that you've done a role play provided for you, come up with one of your own. It may reflect an actual experience, perhaps one in which you felt your response was not particularly effective. Or your role play may reflect a situation you anticipate with a certain amount of dread or uneasiness. Set up the situation for your teammates, giving as much detail as you like, and then do a 1-minute role play around it. Have one of your team members act as observer and note her or his observations on the De-Escalation Feedback Form. Afterwards, discuss the dynamics of the interaction with your teammates for a few minutes."

Student Success Goal

- Minimum of 12 out of 21 possible points as outlined on De-Escalation Feedback Form from Drill 1

To Decrease Difficulty

- N/A

To Increase Difficulty

- N/A

ASSERTIVENESS/CONFRONTATION SKILLS

Like De-Escalation, Assertiveness/Confrontation consists of verbal, nonverbal, and psychological skills. These skills, however, have been developed specifically for use with sexual assailants during the testing stage (Stage 2) of a sexual assault. Competence in these skills enables a defender to interrupt and confound an attacker's effort to intimidate and dominate the defender.

Begin a discussion of Assertiveness/Confrontation with a quick review of the three general stages of sexual assault—selection, testing, physical force (see Step 1, Awareness). Recall with your students the manner in which an assailant engages a potential victim in some kind of interaction in order to determine the likelihood of being able to act out fantasies of dominance and control (Stage 2). Note that the techniques used in Assertiveness/Confrontation make it difficult for an assailant to establish the psychological dominance that leads to physical assault (Stage 3). Explain that these techniques—erect, balanced posture; eye contact; firm voice; and clear, unequivocal verbal messages—represent the potential victim's firm and direct refusal to comply with behaviors the assailant expects of a victim (e.g., fear, deference, naïveté, tentativeness, timidity, compliance) and, in effect, interrupt the assailant's efforts to establish dominance.

When you have defined Assertiveness/Confrontation and identified the kinds of situations in which it may be useful, discuss how to confront by presenting the nonverbal and verbal principles of this strategy (see Figure 3.3). When presenting the nonverbal principles, point out to students that, although essentially the same as the nonverbal principles of De-Escalation, there is a slight difference in the first principle. Instead of presenting a confident and attentive demeanor, as is appropriate when trying to calm down an agitated person, the potential victim of a sexual assault should present a confident and vigilant demeanor. Whereas *attentiveness* sug-

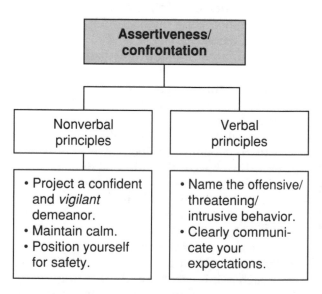

Figure 3.3 Assertiveness/confrontation.

gests a solicitousness that would be inappropriate in a sexual assault, *vigilance* conveys the firmness and attitude of suspicion that suggests to an assailant that this person is lousy victim material.

After you have reviewed the nonverbal principles and the two verbal principles of Confrontation, have your students do the Assertiveness/Confrontation Drills.

Assertiveness/Confrontation Drills

1. Role Playing/Bus Stop Scene
[Corresponds to *Self-Defense*, Step 3,
Assertiveness/Confrontation Drill 1]

Group Management Tips

- Divide your group into teams of three and have them divide up among three roles: a potential sexual assailant, a potential victim, and an observer. *Note:* Feel free to have either gender play either offender or defender. This can provide some startling and useful insights to participants regarding the way in which conditioned responses in women and men often set them up to be sexual aggressors or victims. Keep in mind that some of your students likely have been victims of sexual assault, and, as a result, may find these drills difficult. Remind those students that they have the option of modifying it in some way (i.e., changing a "too familiar" aspect of it, such as environment or language used by the potential attacker), selecting the person with whom they act it out, or just observing this role play.
- You may want to play the attacker yourself. If you do, pause as often as you need to during the role play to praise examples of strong, unequivocal nonverbal and verbal behaviors and to gently encourage the defender if she or he is faltering. Follow their cues; let the defenders control the pace, intensity, and content of the role play as much as possible.
- Instruct those playing assailants to back off at that point in the role play when they feel thoroughly frustrated in the attempt to establish psychological dominance and control. No role play should extend beyond 1 minute.

- After the sexual assailant backs off, have the team sit down and discuss the interaction. At this point, the observer can provide feedback to the defender regarding posture, stance, demeanor, voice tones, use of the two verbal principles of confrontation, and so on. Suggest that your students take no more than 3 minutes for feedback and discussion.
- Repeat the role play three times so that each person plays each role. Be sure to allow time for a 3-minute team discussion following each role play.
- When all role playing is completed, bring the entire group back together for a general discussion.
- Finish by encouraging your students to see these principles as a guide and not as an absolute set of rules. Remind them of the importance of relying on their own finely honed intuitions in determining the best response in these situations.

Equipment

- Sufficient copies of the Assertiveness/Confrontation Feedback Form to distribute 3 or 4 to each group

Instructions and Cues to Class

- "Now you will have the opportunity to practice assertiveness/confrontation skills in a role play of 1 minute or less. One of you will play a potential sexual assailant and attempt to establish psychological dominance and control. Another will play

Assertiveness/Confrontation Feedback Form

<u>Nonverbal Behaviors</u> *(Gain 1 point each)*

Assume a confident and vigilant demeanor.

_____ Eyes on other person's eyes?

_____ Facial expression neutral?

_____ Posture relaxed and alert?

_____ Movement minimized?

Maintain calm.

_____ Breathing deeply and slowly?

_____ Using positive self-talk?

Position yourself for safety.

_____ Distance of 2 arms'-lengths?

_____ Body angled at 45 degrees?

_____ Hands free and in front of body?

_____ Using available barriers?

<u>Verbal Behaviors</u> *(Gain 4 points each)*

_____ Name the offensive or threatening
behavior?

_____ Clearly communicate expectations?

Your Score = _____ nonverbal points + _____ verbal points = _____ total points

defender and attempt to confound the assailant's efforts by applying the principles and techniques we've discussed. The third member of your team will be an observer and provide feedback at the conclusion of the role play on your use of these techniques."

- "Here is the role play:

Bus Stop Scene Revisited

A female is waiting for a bus late one afternoon in a relatively busy section of town. A male approaches, ostensibly to wait for the same bus, and engages her in conversation. After a number of casual questions, he begins to ask more pointed questions about where and with whom she lives. He also begins to move uncomfortably close to her, even touching her shoulder a couple of times. As his questions become more intrusive and personal, her uneasiness grows.

- "Begin this role play on my cue. The role play is over as soon as the potential sexual assailant feels it is useless to continue to try to establish dominance and backs off. When that happens, have a team discussion of the dynamics of the interaction, noting what worked especially well or not at all."

"Begin now."

Student Options

- N/A

Student Success Goal

- Minimum of 15 out of 18 possible points

To Decrease Difficulty

- N/A

To Increase Difficulty

- N/A

2. *Role Playing/Date Rape*
[Corresponds to *Self-Defense*, Step 3, Assertiveness/Confrontation Drill 2]

Group Management Tips

- Gather your group together to discuss application of Assertiveness/Confrontation to date rape situations. Be sure to discuss the data from Burkhart and Stanton (1988) and Koss (1985) that is presented in *Self-Defense*, Step 3, p. 33.
- Use the same format described for earlier role plays. Note that one student will play attacker, one will play defender, and one will observe, using the Assertiveness/Confrontation Feedback Form provided with the Bus Stop Scene.
- Note suggestions in Drill 1 for working with sexual assault survivors in your class who may have difficulty participating in this role play.

Equipment

- Sufficient copies of the Assertiveness/Confrontation Feedback Form to distribute 3 or 4 to each group

Instructions and Cues to Class

- "When you have determined which of you is playing the intended victim, the sexual assailant, and observer, act out this situation:

Date Rape Scene

The defender, a female, is invited by a male friend to play backgammon in his dorm room. On one previous occasion the two have studied together. However, the defender thinks of this person not as a romantic interest, but as a "buddy."

Midway through the game, the potential date rapist, who has been drinking, moves closer to the defender. Abruptly, he begins to touch her face and shoulder in an intimate manner. She tries to draw his attention back to the backgammon game and tells him she's not interested in an intimate relationship with him.

He ignores her and continues to press. She realizes that there's no one else at the end of the hallway and that stereos are blaring at the other end. He grabs her tightly and laughs when she struggles to free herself."

- "Defender, use Assertiveness/Confrontation techniques to deliver a clear, direct, determined, and unambiguous verbal and psychological refusal. For instance, while incorporating all of the nonverbal principles we've discussed, you might say, loudly and firmly, 'Your behavior is aggressive and totally out-of-line. Now let go of me immediately!' or 'What you are doing is assaultive and illegal. Now let me out of here this instant!' When the message is clear and strong enough, the potential date rapist backs off.

"After the assailant backs off, spend a few minutes discussing the interaction with your team and hearing the observer's feedback.

- "Begin now."

Student Options

- N/A

Student Success Goal

- Minimum of 15 out of 18 possible points using same chart used in Bus Stop Scene, Drill 1

To Decrease Difficulty

- N/A

To Increase Difficulty

- N/A

SELF-DEFENSE

Explain to your students during your first class meeting that the final option on the Continuum of Response is Self-Defense. This strategy of last resort is defined here as a response to physical aggression involving self-defense tactics. Emphasize that this strategy comes into play only when all efforts at avoiding or preventing physical aggression fail (see Figure 3.4).

In discussing how to defend oneself, point out that the general rule of thumb is to do whatever is necessary to break free of the attacker and get to safety. Remind students that research suggests that *immediate and vigorous* resistance correlates with deterrence of unarmed attackers.

At this point, raise the issue of the legal and ethical responsibilities of defenders by discussing the ethic of least harm—commitment to using the least damaging or punishing techniques necessary to deter an attacker while still doing whatever is required to insure one's own safety. Suggest to your students that this makes sense not only ethically, but legally and practically as well. For instance, most state laws require that defenders use only that degree of force that is necessary and reasonable, given the situation. And, practically speaking, the use of excessive force by the defender often keeps them in range of the attacker (and consequently at risk) longer than necessary or may anger and incite the attacker to even greater violence.

Explain to your students that they will be learning and practicing a wide variety of self-defense techniques during this course of study. Initially, the focus will be on neutralizing techniques, such as evasions and blocks. The focus will then shift to counterattacks—strikes and kicks that discourage further aggressive action by the attacker. Once both these defensive and offensive foundational skills have been mastered, students will learn how to apply them to a number of common attacks.

Explain that throughout this skill-building process, emphasis will be on learning correct and effective technique and on implementing these techniques in a strategic, effective, and spirited manner.

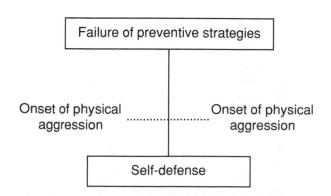

Figure 3.4 Self-defense: The last resort.

Step 4   Evasive Sidestep

In this step, your students will be learning the language of self-defense at the same time that they master their first self-defense skill, an evasive sidestep. As you first present this fairly simple technique, take the time to clearly and carefully define and then use terms such as *neutralizing technique*, *evasions*, *critical distance zone* (CDZ), *defensive posture*, *defensive stance*, *guard*, and *centerline* (see Figure 4.1). Make certain that students understand that this technique is one form of *evasion*, used when the defender needs to get around the attacker to get to an exit.

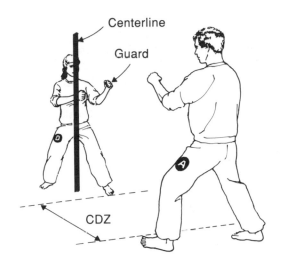

Figure 4.1   The proper defensive stance.

Though the act of sidestepping is not, in itself, difficult for most students, many are challenged by the sense of range and timing required to do this technique effectively. As your students practice, continually draw their attention to the fact that this technique is done in response to attacks from *outside* the CDZ and that it is less likely to work as a response to an attack from inside the CDZ. Also, attend to their timing, making sure that movement off the connecting line is neither too soon (such that they can be "tracked") or too late (such that they can be grabbed or struck by the attacker). By presenting an evasion as the first self-defense technique, you reinforce the notion that, if at all possible, avoidance of physical contact is almost always the defender's initial objective, even after an attack is launched.

STUDENT KEYS TO SUCCESS

- Assume a technically correct defensive stance.
- Lunge step directly to the side just before impact (i.e., stepping with left foot when stepping to left, with right foot when stepping to the right).
- Step rapidly forward toward exit.
- Retreat to safety, or instantly resume defensive stance.

Evasive Sidestep Rating

BEGINNING LEVEL	SKILLED LEVEL
Preparation	
• Body is angled too much (so that student is presenting his or her side), or too little (so that centerline is overexposed).	• Body is angled at 45 degrees, with weight evenly distributed over both feet.
• Feet are too close together.	• Feet are 1-1/2 shoulder-widths apart, providing a solid base of support.
• Centerline is exposed. Guard is too high or too low, with hands resting on the chest.	• Guard covers the centerline from throat to upper abdomen and is correctly positioned in front of body.
• Posture is crouched and tense. Knees are locked, giving a stiff and immobile appearance.	• Posture is erect, yet relaxed. Knees are slightly bent.
• Wrists are hyperextended, with fists clenched and turned palm-in.	• Wrist line is straight, and hands are loosely fisted with little-finger edge toward the attacker.
Execution	
• Sidestep is poorly timed, so that defender moves too soon or too late.	• Defender sidesteps just before impact.
• Sidestep is short and weak.	• Defender bounds to the side, covering roughly 3 or more feet (see Figure 4.2).
• Defender pauses between step to the side and step forward. Feeling is one of "walking-through" technique.	• Defender bounds forward, without pause, following sidestep. Feeling is one of "running-through" technique.
Follow-Up	
• Defender is slow to resume defensive stance, if unable to retreat to safety.	• Defender instantly resumes defensive stance, if unable to retreat to safety.

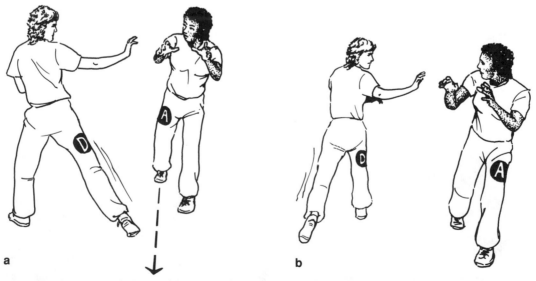

a b

Figure 4.2 During an evasive sidestep, the student should (a) lunge to the side just before impact and (b) step to the left with the left foot (or to the right with the right foot, when evading to the right) and step forward with the other foot toward the escape route.

Error Detection and Correction for Evasive Sidestep

First attend to each student's defensive stance. Check for correct angling, weight distribution, posture, and proper guard. The student's general appearance in this stance should suggest a readiness to move quickly and in any direction.

During the sidestep, look primarily for timing errors, such as a student moving too soon or too late and consequently being tracked or struck. The problem may have to do with a student's difficulty in monitoring an attacker's advance down the connecting line or an inability to move quickly enough to avoid a collision. Also, watch for "dropped guards," which expose the centerline and increase risk.

ERROR

CORRECTION

ERROR	CORRECTION
1. The defending student is moving prematurely and is easily tracked by the attacking student.	1. Advise the defending student to hold his or her ground until the attacker is about 1-1/2 arm's-lengths away and then bound quickly to the side.
2. The defender waits too long before sidestepping and is struck by the attacker.	2. Have the defender initiate the sidestep the instant the attacker lunges forward. Suggest that they bound—not simply step—to the side.
3. Defender's guard drops as he or she sidesteps.	3. Have student focus on maintaining a guard (i.e., keeping both fists and nearly vertical forearms between him- or herself and the attacker) until he or she is completely out of range.

Evasive Sidestep Drills

1. Solo Sidestep Drill
[Corresponds to *Self-Defense*, Step 4, Drill 1]

Group Management and Safety Tips

- Have students spread out and face large, full-length mirrors. Be sure that each has about 6 feet of space on all sides.
- Have students critique and correct their own defensive stances.
- Have all students first practice evasive sidesteps to the left (9:00).
- Have them do 6 or so on your command in order to establish a reasonable pace and reduce the likelihood of students colliding with one another.
- Then have them do approximately 25 additional repetitions on their own.
- Once this has been done, have the group work on evasive sidesteps to the right (3:00). (As before, establish a pace by having

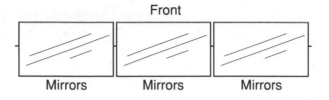

Front

| Mirrors | Mirrors | Mirrors |

⊢ 6 ft. ⊣

students move on your command for the first 5-10 repetitions, and then provide sufficient time for an additional 25 repetitions to be done on their own.)

- Be alert for slippery floors or uneven surfaces on which someone could trip.
- Monitor the group continuously to insure that students are maintaining sufficient space between one another in order to avoid collisions.
- Remove chalk or tape from floor after class is over (if you use increased difficulty drill).

Equipment

- Mirrored wall
- Chalk or tape (for increased difficulty drill)

Instructions and Cues to Class

- "Assume a defensive stance in front of the mirror. Working from the ground up and from the centerline out, make sure that all aspects of your stance are correct."
- "Work for a feeling of suddenness and explosiveness as you practice evasive sidesteps, first to the left and then, on my cue, to the right. Keep posture erect, knees slightly bent, and weight evenly distributed over both feet in order to be able to move quickly in any direction."

- "Monitor your guard before and during your sidestep. As you step to the side, be sure to shift your guard so as to keep it between your centerline and your imaginary attacker."

Student Options

- N/A

Student Success Goals

- 25 correctly executed sidesteps to the left
- 25 correctly executed sidesteps to the right

To Decrease Difficulty

- Do fewer repetitions in each direction.

To Increase Difficulty

- Increase the number of repetitions in each direction.
- Increase the distance covered when sidestepping. To do this, place a mark on the floor with chalk or tape after the initial effort to show the distance covered. Then add a mark showing 1 additional inch, then 2 . . . up to 12 inches. Encourage skilled students to increase distance with each effort and to note the maximal distance covered as Initial Distance Plus _____.

2. Triangle Drill Variations

[Corresponds to *Self-Defense*, Step 4, Drills 2-4]

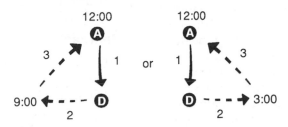

a. Sidestep to defenders left   b. Sidestep to defenders right

Group Management and Safety Tips

- Have each student select a partner. The entire group then forms two parallel lines, with partners assuming a defensive stance and facing one another at a distance of approximately 2 arms'-lengths (just outside the CDZ).
- Make sure that there is plenty of room between pairs to insure that people will not run into one another as they practice sidesteps. Six feet between pairs should be sufficient.
- Have all defenders move left for the first 25 or so repetitions. Advise students to wait for your verbal cue before they practice right evasive sidesteps. This should minimize the likelihood of students colliding with one of the pair practicing next to them.
- Have students reverse attacker and defender roles after the first has completed his or her 25 left evasive sidesteps. When the second of the pair has completed 25 left evasive sidesteps, roles are again reversed and the original defender now practices 25 right evasive sidesteps. The second of the pair then finishes with 25 right evasive sidesteps. All role reversals (defender/attacker) and direction changes should be done on your verbal cue in order to keep movement flowing in generally the same direction and to minimize collisions.
- If you have an odd number of students, you'll need to fill in as an attacker. Try to position yourself so you can do the drill while still monitoring the entire group. You do not need to play the defender, so you'll have a bit of a split focus only half the time.
- Watch that students maintain sufficient distance between pairs at all times so they can leap and bound without fear of landing on another student.

- When doing the Student Options, have students sidestep in either direction. Be sure there is still sufficient space between pairs. (You may have to limit the number of pairs on the floor at one time for these two drill variations.) If half your group is waiting to use the floor, have them spend this time critiquing their own and their partners' defensive stances.

Instructions and Cues to Class

- "Defenders, nod to your partner to signal your readiness to defend against attack. Attackers, when you see your partner nod, charge down the connecting line with your arms outstretched."
- "Defenders, when the attacker has almost reached you, bound to the left with an evasive sidestep. Follow immediately with a step toward 12:00 or behind your attacker. Turn and face the attacker, assume a defensive stance, and prepare to signal your readiness for another attack. You'll be repeating this approximately 25 times. I'll tell you when to stop and reverse roles, and later when to switch to right evasive sidesteps. Keep in mind that all attacks come at the defender's nod."

Student Options

- "After you've done the standard Triangle Drill, attackers can shout as they charge down the connecting line. This lets the defender work on moving quickly into action despite being startled or confused by a noisy attack. Do 25 repetitions, and then switch roles." [Corresponds to *Self-Defense*, Step 4, Drill 3]

- "After you've done the standard Triangle Drill, and have then added a shout (see preceding Student Option), you can do yet another variation on this drill. This variation allows the *attacker* to decide when the attack takes place, rather than having the defender initiate each exchange with a nod. The attacker can charge at any moment after a completed exchange (i.e., after partners turn to face one another again and make eye contact). This helps the defender learn to recover quickly from one attack and prepare to respond to another attack at any moment. Do 25 repetitions, and then switch roles." [Corresponds to *Self-Defense*, Step 4, Drill 4]

Student Success Goals

Regular Triangle Drill
- 25 successful evasive sidesteps to the left
- 25 successful evasive sidesteps to the right

Triangle Drill With Shout (Student Option)
- 25 successful evasive sidesteps in either direction

Triangle Drill With Spontaneous Attack (Student Option)
- 25 successful evasive sidesteps in either direction

To Decrease Difficulty

- Slow down the attacks. Give the defender plenty of time to set up and prepare for each attack.

To Increase Difficulty

- Speed up attacks. Have attackers move more quickly down the connecting line.
- Have attacker vary the speed of the attack and the range from which it is launched. (*Note:* All attacks should still come from outside the CDZ, but rather than the attacker always starting at precisely 2 arms'-lengths, she or he might start at 3 or even 4 arms'-lengths.) The defender would still wait until the very last instant to move in order to avoid being tracked. By responding to attacks launched from varying distances and at different velocities, the defender can further hone his or her sense of timing and range.

3. *Milling Drill*
[Corresponds to *Self-Defense*, Step 4, Drill 5]

Group Management and Safety Tips

- Have four or more students spread out so that there is a minimum distance of 2 arms'-lengths between them.
- Students will mill randomly and rapidly around the room, maintaining critical distance between themselves and all other students.
- Any student can be an attacker by shouting "You!" while pointing at another student. Both attacker and defender freeze for an instant after eye contact is made. Then the attacker rushes down the connecting line with arms outstretched as if to grab or shove the defender. The defender sidesteps at the appropriate moment. Both then begin to mill again until one is moved to attack or called on to defend.
- Suggest to students that attacks be slower during the first 30 seconds of the drill, and increase in speed and intensity as everyone becomes more comfortable with the drill format.
- Advise students to be aware of one another and avoid collisions. Point out that a decision about whether to step right or left may depend on whether a third person is currently occupying the space to their immediate left or right.

Instructions and Cues to Class

- "As you are milling around, maintain a distance of 2 arms'-lengths from everyone else."
- "Anyone can be an attacker. Simply stop, point at the person you want to attack, and loudly shout, 'You.' As soon as he or she stops and makes eye contact with you, charge."
- "If you are attacked, sidestep and move behind your attacker as you did in the Triangle Drill. Then immediately resume milling."
- "Avoid running into one another inadvertently. Try to be conscious of everyone involved in the drill, and maintain critical distance at all times."

Student Options

- N/A

Student Success Goal

- 2 minutes of effective sidesteps in response to charging attacks while milling

To Decrease Difficulty

- Advise students to slow attacks down and allow more time for defenders to prepare for the attack when it has been called.
- Limit this drill to 30 seconds of milling. Allow participants to rest for 1 minute, then mill around for another 30 seconds.

To Increase Difficulty

- Instruct students to charge more quickly down the connecting line. Have attackers allow less time for defenders to prepare for their attack, by beginning the charge as soon as they have shouted "You."
- Extend drill to 3-5 minutes. Milling constantly, maintaining the vigilance necessary to keep 2 arms'-lengths from everyone else, and executing effective sidesteps while increasingly fatigued is quite challenging.

Step 5 Blocks

Now that your students know how to evade an attack launched from outside the critical distance zone (CDZ), they are ready to learn how to block an attack that comes from inside the CDZ. In this step, they will practice deflecting incoming strikes to either side of their centerlines using either an outside block or an inside block.

Initially, have your students concentrate on the biomechanical details of these two blocks—correct positioning of the guard at the start of the technique, the use of trunk rotation to power the block, last-minute rotation of the forearm to a palm-out or palm-in position while moving it either away from or across the centerline, tightening of the fist at the last instant, and a quick return to the guard position.

After mastering the technical execution of both blocks, your students will be ready to practice them in response to attacks thrown by a practice partner. The challenges of timing and range posed by partner work will hone and sharpen your students' observational skills. Encourage use of a "soft" and receptive vision (i.e., taking in the entire visual field—similar to looking at a distant horizon) and awareness of the general monitoring points (e.g., hips and shoulders). As students become more effective in reading intention, they can practice application of these blocks in the increasingly spontaneous and unpredictable drills provided.

In these application drills, watch for correct timing and placement of the block. Incoming attacks should be intercepted by the time that they have covered approximately 2/3 of the distance to the target. Make sure that your students are consistently deflecting wrist-to-wrist and using mirror-image blocks (i.e., the blocking arm is immediately opposite the attacking limb). Have the practice partners of your most skilled students gradually increase the speed of attack in order to further improve skilled students' concentration and quick response.

In Drills 4 and 5, be sure to address the criteria for choosing either the inside or outside block by discussing angles of attack, intended follow-up to the block, and possible avenues of escape.

STUDENT KEYS TO SUCCESS

- Prepare to block by assuming a defensive stance.
- Power the block with a slight rotation of the body.
- Sweep a vertical forearm to the side (for outside block) or across centerline toward the opposite shoulder (for inside block).
- Block wrist-to-wrist and mirror-image.
- Intercept the punch 2/3 of the way to the target, and deflect away from the centerline.
- Retreat to safety or maintain a defensive stance.

Blocks Rating

BEGINNING LEVEL	SKILLED LEVEL
Preparation	
• Feet are close together, resulting in a high, narrow stance	• Feet are 1-1/2 shoulder-widths apart, so that student appears grounded and centered
• Guard is held in palm-in position	• Palms are facing one another, with ulnar edge of wrist directed toward partner
• Defender's eyes are trained on attacker's fists rather than on the attacker's eyes	• Eyes are on attacker's eyes
• Defender exhibits signs of nervousness (e.g., constantly shifting weight from one foot to the other, clenching/unclenching fists, vision darting and unfocused)	• Defender's body is still, gaze is directed steadily toward attacker; defender appears calm, focused, prepared to take quick defensive action
Execution	
• Defender impacts with surfaces other than the forearm	• Defender consistently intercepts wrist-to-wrist on both inside and outside blocks (see Figure 5.1)
• Interception is attempted either too soon or too late, either because of sluggish "reading" of the attack or slow movement time	• Incoming attack is intercepted 2/3 of distance to target
• Little indication of an established motor pattern that would insure quick and effective deflection of incoming strikes	• Blocks are increasingly reflexive, suggesting an established motor pattern

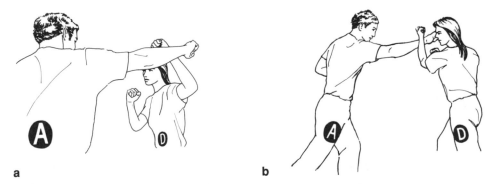

a   b

Figure 5.1   The proper technique for (a) an outside block and (b) an inside block.

Error Detection and Correction for Blocks

First check out your students' readiness to respond by correcting any errors in their defensive stances. Note where they are looking and whether they appear to be calm and alert.

The most common technical errors are

- failure to maintain a consistent guard,
- using something other than the ulnar edge of the forearm to intercept the attack, and
- using a cross-body rather than mirror-image block.

Finally, watch for errors in timing (i.e., blocks coming too soon or too late to deflect an attack and keep from being hit).

ERROR   **CORRECTION**

1. Defender's centerline is frequently exposed to attack.

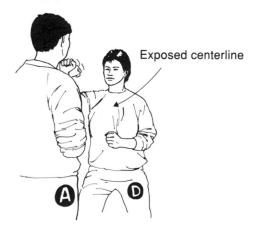

Exposed centerline

1. Advise the defender to maintain proper guard at all times. Remind him or her to keep the nonblocking arm directly in front of the centerline, even while using the other arm to block. Encourage quick returns of the blocking arm to a guard position.

2. Defender is blocking too soon or too late or with the wrong hand.

2. Defender's monitoring skills need sharpening. Review the indications that an attacker is about to launch a strike. Include both obvious cues (hip or shoulder movement) and subtle cues (change in expression, slight shift in guard, or increased tension in attacker's body). Encourage an inclusive vision, in which defenders are as aware of the edges of their visual field as they are of the center. (The visual "feeling" is similar to that of looking at the horizon.)

Blocking Drills

1. Solo Blocking Drill

[Corresponds to *Self-Defense*, Step 5, Drill 1]

Group Management and Safety Tips

- Have students array themselves in front of a large full-length mirror and assume correct defensive stances.
- Have students first practice outside blocks, using the mirror to monitor their form. Then have them practice the same block with their eyes closed. Repeat doing inside blocks.
- Be sure each student has sufficient room to practice blocking and can easily see her or his reflection in the mirror.

Equipment

- Mirrored wall

Instructions and Cues to Class

- "The purpose of this drill is to begin to develop a feel for these blocks, without the additional challenges of timing and range that are introduced with partner work."
- "Assume a correct defensive stance in front of the mirror. Begin throwing half-speed outside blocks, alternating right and left. Closely monitor all of the details of the execution phase. Finish each block with a rapid return to the guard position."

- "Now try this with your eyes closed. Get a feel for moving your arm only as far as would be necessary to knock an incoming strike off the connecting line and away from your body. Make a rapid return to a protective guard a part of your block."
- "Now do the same with inside blocks."

Student Options

- N/A

Student Success Goals

- 20 outside blocks with eyes open
- 20 outside blocks with eyes closed
- 20 inside blocks with eyes open
- 20 inside blocks with eyes closed

To Decrease Difficulty

- Drill is already in simplest form

To Increase Difficulty

- Gradually increase the speed of blocks until you have reached your top speed without sacrificing correct form.
- See how many well executed blocks you can throw in 30 seconds.

2. Predictable Punch Drill

[Corresponds to *Self-Defense*, Step 5, Drill 2]

Group Management and Safety Tips

- Have each student select a partner. The entire group then forms two parallel lines, with partners assuming a defensive stance and facing one another at a distance of just under 2 arms'-lengths.
- If you have an odd number of students, you'll need to fill in as the attacker for the unpartnered student. Position yourself so that you can do this while still monitoring the activity of the entire group. Because you are only playing attacker, you can throw a

few punches to be blocked, pause to watch the group, and then return to work with your partner. When the remainder of your group switches roles, you will continue playing attacker. In this way, your partner will eventually have the opportunity to respond to the same number of punches as the others, despite the need for you to periodically leave her or him in order to provide feedback and attention to others.
- Have attackers throw half-speed punches, alternating hands in a predictable pattern.

Be sure that attackers are not throwing so fast or so deep that they will hit a defender whose block is unsuccessful.

- Be sure that there is sufficient space—a minimum of 3 or 4 feet—between pairs in order to insure that none of your students are hit by someone practicing next to them.
- Remind your students that, at this stage, attackers should be doing something called *working harmony* with partners, rather than engaging in any kind of competitive play. They should not be trying to confuse defenders by throwing fakes and feints. Rather, they should launch clean punches along a clearly discernible trajectory and at a speed that is appropriate to the defender's skill. This harmonious manner of working together minimizes frustration and injuries among novices and hastens and improves the learning of blocking skills.
- Advise defenders to block lightly in order to spare *both* partners' forearms.

Instructions and Cues to Class

- "In this drill, you'll be testing your blocking skills against an incoming strike thrown by your partner. You must block your partner's punch before his or her fist has traveled 2/3 of the way to your nose."
- "Attackers will alternate right and left punches in a predictable pattern so that defenders don't have to guess which hand they must use to deflect, and can instead concentrate on executing technically correct blocks at precisely the right instant. The

first few punches should be thrown at half-speed. As defenders' proficiency improves, attackers can speed up their punches."

- "First work on outside blocks only. When you have reached your success goal for outside blocks, switch to inside blocks."

Student Option

- "Attackers, start with half-speed punches, then gradually increase speed as the defender's blocks become more reflexive. Continually adjust speed to insure that you are providing a reasonable challenge for your partner, while not overwhelming him or her."

Student Success Goals

- 42 out of 50 total punches blocked successfully and correctly with an outside block:
  21 out of 25 right outside blocks
  21 out of 25 left outside blocks
- 42 out of 50 total punches blocked successfully and correctly with an inside block:
  21 out of 25 right inside blocks
  21 out of 25 left inside blocks

To Decrease Difficulty

- Slow punches down.
- Have attacker pause longer between punches.
- Increase speed more gradually.

To Increase Difficulty

- Increase the speed of punches.
- Shorten the pause between punches.

3. Monitoring Drill
[Corresponds to *Self-Defense*, Step 5, Drill 3]

Group Management and Safety Tips

- Have practice partners face one another in defensive stances so that the entire class forms two parallel lines.
- For 2 or 3 minutes, have designated defenders shout as soon as they perceive the attacker's intention to punch. Emphasize to your students the necessity of "soft vision" in order to read the attacker's intention at the earliest possible instant. Remind them

that their vision should be inclusive and that they should be as aware of the periphery of their visual field as of the center of the field.

- Invite ideas on what might constitute signals on the part of the attacker that suggest a punch is imminent (e.g., a change in attacker's expression, shift of his or her guard, increased tension in the body, movement of the hips or shoulders).

- Have attackers confirm or deny that they were about to punch by saying "yes" or "no."
- After 2 or 3 minutes, have partners switch roles so that attackers are now defenders and defenders are attackers.

Instructions and Cues to Class

- "The purpose of this drill is to improve your ability to read an attacker's intention to punch at the earliest possible moment."
- "Defenders, stand facing your partner in a defensive stance. Assume a soft, receptive vision that takes in the attacker's entire body without focusing hard on any part of it."
- "When you think your partner is about to punch, shout 'Now!' Attackers, instantly abort the punch, if it was launched at all."
- "After a number of consecutive efforts in which you've accurately predicted your partner's intention to punch, try identifying the side the punch is coming from by shouting 'Left!' or 'Right!'"

Student Options

- N/A

Student Success Goals

- 20 out of 25 successful readings of attacker's intention to punch as evidenced by defender shouting "Now!" before punch has traveled halfway to target
- 20 out of 25 successful readings of attacker's intention to throw a left or right punch as evidenced by defender's shouting "Left!" or "Right!" before the punch has traveled halfway to target

To Decrease Difficulty

- Advise attacker to move more slowly, and make little (if any) effort to disguise intention to punch.

To Increase Difficulty

- Advise attacker to minimize telegraphing of intention to punch. Movement should be explosive and quick.
- Rotate partners so that defenders have to "read" a number of different attackers.

4. *Unpredictable Punch Drill*
[Corresponds to *Self-Defense*, Step 5, Drills 4-6]

Group Management and Safety Tips

- Have practice partners face one another in defensive stances as in previous drills.
- Instruct attackers to throw half-speed punches in no particular order (i.e., not alternating).
- Instruct defenders to use monitoring skills to determine which arm an attacker will use, and then throw a correctly executed mirror-image block.
- Have students concentrate first on outside blocks, and then, on your cue, switch to inside blocks.
- Make certain that each pair of partners has plenty of space (e.g., 4 feet between pairs) in which to work.
- Advise defenders to keep their blocks light, in order to spare both partners' forearms.
- Advise attackers not to resist the force of the block, but rather to go with it.

Instructions and Cues to Class

- "Defenders, in this drill you will be blocking random order punches with mirror-image blocks. Maintain a soft, receptive vision in order to identify the likely attacking arm, then move quickly to intercept the attack before it is 2/3 of the way to your nose. Remain focused and alert throughout this drill, and work constantly to improve both your perceptual and movement skills."
- "Attackers, throw your punches in a regular cadence but in no particular order. Start slowly, and then gradually build up speed. Over the course of this drill, work to eliminate any extraneous movement that might telegraph your intention to attack."
- "First use outside blocks. When you have reached your success goal for outside blocks, switch to inside blocks."

Student Options

- "When you are comfortable blocking random order punches thrown in a regular cadence, have your partner throw random punches in a broken rhythm. First work on outside blocks, and then inside blocks." [Corresponds to *Self-Defense*, Step 5, Drill 5, Broken Rhythm Drill]
- "For 3 minutes, use either an outside or an inside block to deflect incoming punches, thrown in random order and in a broken rhythm. All blocks, whether inside or outside, should be mirror-image blocks. Each time you block, freeze in the completed block position for an instant and identify the angle—whether that of safety (inside block) or opportunity (outside block). Keep in mind that the more protective inside block lends itself to a quick retreat, whereas the outside block is frequently used in combination with counterattacks (follow-up strikes thrown by the defender). Note that your choice as to whether to use an outside or inside block is determined not only by your intended follow-up, but also by the angle of attack and by the precise placement of your own guard in relation to the incoming punch. In other words, you simply may be positioned to do one block more easily than the other." [Corresponds to *Self-Defense*, Step 5, Drill 6, Variable Block Drill]

Student Success Goals

Unpredictable Punch Drill

- 40 out of 50 random order punches blocked correctly with outside blocks
- 40 out of 50 random order punches blocked correctly with inside blocks

Broken Rhythm Drill (Student Option)

- 40 out of 50 random order punches blocked correctly with outside blocks
- 40 out of 50 random order punches blocked correctly with inside blocks

Variable Block Drill (Student Option)

- 3 minutes of continuous blocking using either the outside or the inside block

To Decrease Difficulty

- Decrease speed of random order punches. Advise attacker to do little to disguise intention to punch.

To Increase Difficulty

- Increase speed of random order punches. Advise attacker to minimize telegraphing intentions.

5. *Circle Retreat Drill*
[Corresponds to *Self-Defense*, Step 5, Drill 7]

Group Management and Safety Tips

- This drill is usually done with only two people at a time. However, if you are practicing in a full-size gym, two pairs of students can do this simultaneously.
- Designate one corner of the room as the avenue of escape. Instruct the attacker to take up position between the designated avenue of escape and the defender, facing the defender.
- Instruct the attacker to move slowly but steadily toward the defender while throwing controlled, slow-speed punches. Defender will circle from side to side in order to stay out of range of the punches, taking care to block any that come close enough to land. When the defender has maneuvered close enough to the avenue of escape to be able to reach it before the attacker is able to do so, he or she dashes toward it.
- Be sure that there is plenty of space for the wide circling and rapid direction changes that characterize this drill. Allow more than ample room for each pair of students.
- If you have more than one pair of students practicing at a time, assign others to be spotters, whose job it will be to keep two defenders from backing into or otherwise colliding with one another.
- People awaiting their turns can be instructed to play not-so-innocent bystanders by goading and shouting from the sidelines. This adds considerably to the stress of the defender and should be done only after he or she has practiced the skill a few times and successfully escaped.

- Advise defenders to face forward when they bolt for the exit, *not* to run backwards. As they run toward the avenue of escape, have them glance over their shoulders periodically to determine whether the attacker is in pursuit.

Instructions and Cues to Class

- "The purpose of this drill is to practice defense against a punching attack in which the attacker is rapidly moving toward you."
- "As the attacker advances toward you, move away and to one side to avoid being hit. Change directions as often as necessary to keep the attacker off-balance and out of range. Keep your guard up at all times so that you're in position to block any punches that come within striking distance."
- "Try to maneuver closer to your avenue of escape. As soon as *you* are closer to it than is your attacker, break and run."

Student Option

- "When you are comfortable with the drill, have your attacker shout at you as he or she advances. This adds to the realism of the attack and gives you a chance to practice the skill in a slightly more stressful and chaotic situation."

Student Success Goals

- 3 sets of 15 seconds of a circling retreat with blocks as needed and a dash to safety
- 1 set of 15 seconds of a circling retreat with attacker shouting

To Decrease Difficulty

- Have attacker advance more slowly, throwing very slow punches.
- Eliminate all distractions, such as shouting by the attacker or bystanders.

To Increase Difficulty

- Have attacker advance more quickly and noisily.
- Restrict the area allowed the defender for circling and maneuvering into position for a dash to safety.
- Have those students not practicing the skill form a circle around the attacker and the defender. Designate a space between two of those forming the circle to be the avenue of escape. Slowly tighten the circle, constantly reducing the total space available for maneuvering. Stop when the size of the circle does not allow the defender to remain slightly outside the CDZ at all times.

Step 6   Front-Facing Counterattacks

If defensive maneuvers such as evasions, blocks, and hold breaks (to be presented in Steps 9 through 13) are not sufficient to discourage an attacker from pressing an assault, one may be forced to respond with counterattacks. Counterattacks are powerful, ballistic strikes thrown to vulnerable parts of the attacker's body to cause sufficient pain and discomfort to allow the defender time to escape.

In this step, students learn five counterattacks thrown from a front-facing position (face-to-face with an attacker): punch, eye gouge, palm-heel strike, web strike, and front kick.

In the process of learning these techniques, they will also become familiar with body weapons and body targets—the parts of the body (i.e., weapons) used to strike vulnerable areas (targets) on the assailant. Explain that body weapons include

- both arms,
- both legs,
- the head, and
- voice.

Use Figure 6.1 to point out body targets to your students.

STUDENT KEYS TO SUCCESS

- Prepare to counterattack by assuming a defensive stance, with hands in guard position.
- Initiate strike with sharp, short rotation of hips.
- Follow straight-line trajectories for punches, palm-heel strikes, web strikes, and front snap kicks.
- Follow a slightly curved trajectory for eye gouges.
- Maintain correct hand and foot positions for each technique, so that the proper striking surface impacts on the target.
- Aim for precise and appropriate targets for each technique.
- Come from and return to a guard position on every hand technique.
- Retreat to safety or maintain a defensive stance.
- Throughout the movement, maintain balance and alignment and move from larger to smaller muscle groups to generate maximum force with minimum effort.

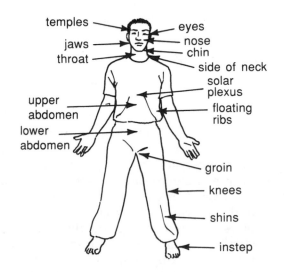

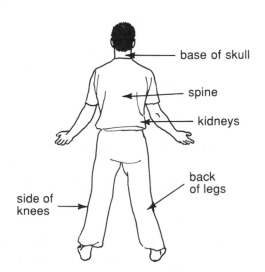

Figure 6.1   Body targets: (a) front view and (b) rear view.

Front-Facing Counterattack Rating

BEGINNING LEVEL	SKILLED LEVEL
General	
• Lacks hip rotation to power hand strikes	• Initiates all strikes by sharp, short hip rotation (trailing hand strikes incorporate slightly greater hip rotation)
• Nonstriking hand dangles loosely by defender's side when other hand is being used to counterattack	• Nonstriking hand is held directly in front of defender's chest and throat during execution to maintain centerline coverage
• Delayed return of striking hand to guard position	• Quick return of striking hand to guard position to protect centerline or to set up for another strike
Punches	
• Strikes with flat of fist or second row of knuckles	• Strikes with top portion of first knuckles of index and middle fingers
• Wrist line bent	• Wrist line straight
• Punch "hooks" to target	• Punch moves along straight-line trajectory
Eye Gouge	
• Two-fingered jab along straight-line trajectory	• Palm and fingers braced in rounded position, following slightly curved trajectory
Palm-Heel Strike	
• Straight wristline results in striking surface of midpalm or even fingers	• Wrist is hyperextended so base of palm impacts attacker's nose or chin
Web Strike	
• Loose, flaccid hand strikes general region of throat	• Hand stiff, webbing between thumb and index finger taut and aimed precisely for Adam's apple
Front Snap Kick	
• Kick lacks chamber/rechamber, targeted imprecisely (leg appears to be flung haphazardly toward attacker's leg)	• Kick is crisply chambered, driven directly toward attacker's knee or midshin, then rapidly rechambered before foot is set back down

Error Detection and Correction for Front-Facing Counterattacks

Errors in front-facing attacks can be avoided by careful attention to

- hand/foot positions (to insure that a well-supported striking surface impacts on the target),
- use of correct strike trajectories (to maximize power and penetration), and
- precise targeting of each technique.

ERROR   **CORRECTION**

Punch

1. Defender is rotating fist to palm-down position prematurely, resulting in "winging" elbows.

1. Have defender rotate wrists at impact or at the end of extension.

2. Defender's wrist is flexed, hyperextended, or bent sideways, so that she or he is at risk of spraining or otherwise injuring the wrist on impact.

2. Have your student concentrate on maintaining an absolutely straight wrist line. If necessary, splint the wrist with a pencil or ruler to keep it from flexing or hyperextending.

Eye Gouge

1. Defender's fingers are either stiff and straight, or too flaccid.

1. Have defender round his or her hand as if holding a large grapefruit. Fingers should be slightly curved and held firmly in position to prevent them from being jammed.

Palm-Heel Strike

1. Defender's wrist is not sufficiently hyperextended to insure that the heel of the hand strikes the target.

1. Have defender hyperextend wrist maximally. Angle should be at least 45 degrees.

ERROR   **CORRECTION**

Web Strike

1. Defender has insufficient tension in hand. Fingers are loose and slightly curved. Thumb is allowed to relax next to index finger.

1. Have defender concentrate on details of the hand position. Hand should be palm down with thumb splayed as far as possible from fingers. Fingers should be locked in extension and pressed together. The narrow leading edge of the webbing between thumb and index finger is the correct striking surface. This rigid hand position assures an effective technique and also prevents injury to the hand.

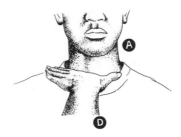

Front Snap Kick

1. Defender's kick lacks a chamber or rechamber.

1. Have defender practice the kick in four counts as follows:

"One"—initiate chamber
"Two"—launch the kick
"Three"—rechamber
"Four"—set foot down

Repeat this drill until student is including both an initial chamber and rechamber. Then have student practice the kick in a single, flowing movement that includes all four segments.

ERROR   **CORRECTION**

2. Defender's foot is dangling loosely at the ankle, resulting in toes rather than the ball of foot impacting on the target.

2. Remind student to tighten and stabilize the foot and ankle at impact to provide a firm striking surface and to prevent injury to the ankle. To get a feel for the correct foot position, have your student roll up onto the balls of the feet (a). This same foot position, maintained during a front kick, insures that the striking surface is the ball of the foot (b).

a

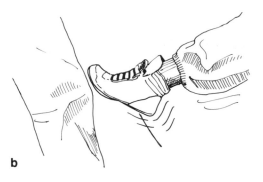

b

Front-Facing Counterattack Drills

1. Mirror Drill

[Corresponds to *Self-Defense*, Step 6, Drill 1]

Group Management and Safety Tips

- Have students stand in front of a large, full-length mirror and assume correct defensive stances.
- Be sure students are spaced approximately 3 feet apart and that each is able to carefully monitor his or her form in the mirror.

- Suggest to students that they stop short of fully extending their arms on hand strikes in order to avoid hyperextending the elbow.
- Suggest to students that they throw kicks at no more than 3/4 speed to avoid hyperextending the knee.

Equipment

- Mirrors along front wall

Instructions and Cues to Class

- "Assume a defensive stance in front of the mirror. Quickly check to see that all aspects of your stance are correct."
- "Moving at slow speed, alternate throwing lead and trailing punches (eye gouges, palm-heel strikes, web strikes, front snap kicks) toward your mirror image."
- "Monitor your centerline coverage, strike trajectory, striking surface, and all other details of your technique. Continue this drill until you have thrown at least 15 lead and 15 reverse punches (eye gouges, palm-heel strikes, web strikes, front snap kicks)."

Student Option

- "When you are consistently throwing correctly executed counterattacks, try throwing a few of each with your eyes closed. Concentrate on balance and on power flowing from your hips through your arms and legs."

Student Success Goals

Punches
- 15 correctly executed lead punches
- 15 correctly executed reverse punches

Eye gouges
- 15 correctly executed gouges with lead hand
- 15 correctly executed gouges with trailing hand

Palm-heel strikes
- 15 correctly executed lead-hand strikes
- 15 correctly executed trailing-hand strikes

Web strikes
- 15 correctly executed lead-hand strikes
- 15 correctly executed trailing-hand strikes

Front snap kicks
- 15 correctly executed lead-leg kicks
- 15 correctly executed trailing-leg kicks

To Decrease Difficulty

- N/A

To Increase Difficulty

- Try to increase the speed of each strike. Work on accelerating technique (i.e., increasing the miles-per-hour speed of the strike as it nears its target). Don't forget to stop short of full extension to avoid hyperextending the elbow.

2. *Rocking Horse Drill*
[Corresponds to *Self-Defense*, Step 6, Drills 2-5]

Group Management and Safety Tips

- Have each student select a partner. Then have the entire group form two parallel lines, with partners facing one another in defensive stances. Designate which side will throw the first punch in this back-and-forth drill.
- Emphasize that all strikes should stop 2 inches short of impact with a partner's body.
- Instruct students to move slowly at first and to concentrate on correct hand position, accurate trajectories, and precise targeting. Advise a slow and steady rhythm, back and forth, like a rocking horse. Plan for approximately 2 minutes for each technique.
- Remind students to adjust their distance from one another when they are ready to begin alternating front snap kicks. They'll need a little more space to insure that they are able to stop 2 inches short of striking their partners' knees or shins.
- To avoid hyperextending elbows, students should stop short of full arm extension on all hand strikes. Front snap kicks can be fully extended, but they should be thrown at about half-speed to avoid stressing the knee. *Note:* There is a risk of joint hyperextension only when techniques are thrown into the air. When there is actual contact with a target (e.g., a punching bag, other heavy bag, or assailant's body), this risk is reduced.

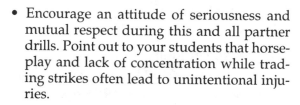

- Encourage an attitude of seriousness and mutual respect during this and all partner drills. Point out to your students that horseplay and lack of concentration while trading strikes often lead to unintentional injuries.

Instructions and Cues to Class

- "Stand facing your partner in a defensive stance. Slowly begin trading punches. Alternate the hand you use each time it is your turn to punch, so that you are doing an equal number of lead- and trailing-hand strikes. Direct your punches precisely to one of four targets: nose, chin, throat, or solar plexus. Stop 2 inches short of impact."
- "When you have thrown 30 punches to varying targets, repeat this exercise using the other four front-facing counterattacks. For all techniques, keep a slow, steady, rhythmic pace—back and forth, like a rocking horse."

Student Options

- "When you've done the standard rocking horse drill in which you concentrate on only one type of counterattack at a time, try throwing whichever of the five counterattacks you like. Try not to use the same technique on two consecutive turns. Keep trading single techniques and giving fairly equal attention to both lead- and trailing-limb counterattacks. Adjust distance from your partner as needed to insure that you are able to stop 2 inches short of contact with their bodies. Monitor all technical aspects of each technique—hand and foot position, appropriate and precise targeting, correct

strike trajectories, and so on." [Corresponds to *Self-Defense*, Step 6, Drill 3]
- "Add a *kiyai* to each of your counterattacks. Before incorporating them into a rocking-horse format, try a few by themselves. Place your hands over your diaphragm and think about this deep, harsh sound coming from your midsection, rather than from your throat. Begin by saying 'hya' in a normal tone. Gradually increase to full volume over a dozen or so repetitions. At full volume, your abdominal muscles should contract powerfully with each effort. Now add a spirited kiyai to each of your strikes or kicks as you and your partner again trade variable front-facing counterattacks." [Corresponds to *Self-Defense*, Step 6, Drill 4]
- "A yet more challenging option consists of building combinations of front-facing counterattacks. Begin by doing two counterattacks, one immediately after the other. Interlock your techniques, that is, launch your second strike as you are retracting the limb used in your first strike. Trade two-technique combinations with your partner for about 30 seconds using the rocking-horse format. Then trade 3-, 4-, and finally 5-strike combinations. Be sure to allow at *least* 30 seconds of practicing 3-strike combos before moving on to 4-strike combos, and so on." [Corresponds to *Self-Defense*, Step 6, Drill 5]

Student Success Goals

Simple Rocking Horse Drill

- 30 punches each to variable targets (15 lead/15 reverse)
- 30 eye gouges (15 lead/15 trailing)

- 30 palm-heel strikes (15 lead/15 trailing)
- 30 web strikes (15 lead/15 trailing)
- 30 front snap kicks (15 lead/15 trailing)

Rocking Horse Variable Strike Drill (Student Option)

- 3 minutes of continuous trading of front-facing strikes

Rocking Horse with Kiyais (Student Option)

- 1 minute of continuous trading of front-facing strikes, each accompanied by a kiyai.

Rocking Horse Combination-Building Drill (Student Option)

- Minimum of 30 seconds of a variety of 2-strike combos
- Minimum of 30 seconds of a variety of 3-strike combos
- Minimum of 30 seconds of a variety of 4-strike combos
- Minimum of 30 seconds of a variety of 5-strike combos

To Decrease Difficulty

Simple Rocking Horse Drill and Variable Strike Drill

- Decrease speed of delivery.
- Increase distance between partners so that there is a space of about 12 inches between one person's almost fully extended limb and his or her partner. This is usually reassuring to students who may be especially anxious about inadvertently hitting or being hit by a partner.

Rocking Horse With Kiyais (Student Option)

- Have student shout "No!" rather than kiyai. This often feels easier and more realistic to students.

Rocking Horse Combination-Building Drill (Student Option)

- Allow students to pause for a few seconds after throwing one technique to consider which additional technique might appropriately follow the first. Encourage them to take the time they need to see which combinations work for them.
- Provide more time for students to work on 2-strike combos before moving on to 3-strike combos, and so on.
- Have students throw all techniques at slow-speed or only as fast as they feel comfortable throwing them.

To Increase Difficulty

- Increase the speed of delivery.
- Have person playing the attacker "react" to each counterattack as if he or she had actually been struck (see Figure 6.2). Keep in mind that "the head always follows pain" in determining how to respond realistically. This play-acting adds to the realism of the practice. It also requires the person throwing counterattacks to make adjustments for a constantly shifting range and the varying accessibility of different body targets. This assumes more developed perceptual and movement skills than those required to throw techniques at a stationary, consistently upright partner.

Figure 6.2   To Increase Difficulty: Have attacker react to each counterattack.

3. Block/Counterattack Drill
[Corresponds to *Self-Defense*, Step 6, Drill 6]

 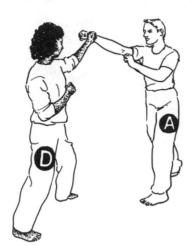 

Group Management and Safety Tips

- Have each student select a partner. Then have the entire group form two parallel lines with partners facing one another in defensive stances, left sides leading.
- Remind attackers to wait until defender has thrown a counterattack before launching another punch. This 1- or 2-second pause will follow each exchange, an exchange consisting of a punch attack, a block, and a counterattack.
- Students can sometimes become a little "spacey" in this drill. Encourage them to stay on-task and to move through the exercises at a reasonably steady pace.

Instructions and Cues to Class

- "In this drill, you'll be combining blocks and counterattacks. Think of the block and counterattack as a unit—a smooth, flowing sequence of moves done in rapid succession."
- "Defenders, you will be assuming a left lead when responding to right punch attacks and a right lead when responding to left punch attacks. Always use your lead arm to block and your trailing arm to counterattack. In this way, the arm nearest the incoming strike deflects it off its path, while the power arm (given greater hip rotation in trailing limb techniques) is reserved for the counterattack."

- "To begin, defenders assume a left lead. Attackers, throw slow-speed right punches toward the defender's nose. Defenders, use a left outside block to deflect the incoming punch to the side, and follow with a right punch counterattack toward your attacker's nose."
- "When you are proficient at left outside block-right counterattack combinations, try a right outside block-left punch counterattack combination. Remember to assume a right leg lead on this."

Student Options

- "When you have practiced punch counterattacks, substitute other front-facing strikes, such as eye gouges, palm-heel strikes, web strikes, and front snap kicks. You will likely find that a kick done from this range is somewhat awkward."
- "Note which hand strikes flow most easily and powerfully following your block."

Student Success Goals

In response to right-handed punch:
- 20 left outside blocks followed by right punches to various punch targets (use left lead)
- 20 left outside blocks followed by any of the 5 front-facing counterattacks, using right hand or foot (left lead)

In response to left-handed punch:

- 20 right outside blocks followed by left punches to various punch targets (use right lead)
- 20 right outside blocks followed by any of the 5 front-facing counterattacks using left hand or foot (right lead)

To Decrease Difficulty

- Slow attacks down. Pause for a few seconds after each exchange to allow defenders sufficient time to prepare for next attack.

To Increase Difficulty

- Have attackers initiate each exchange with *either* a right or left punch. Defenders respond with outside block (mirror-image) and a counterattack. Students should maintain the same stance throughout this drill. Most right-handed defenders will maintain a left lead, whereas left-handed defenders will tend to maintain a right lead. Point out to students that this will require that they sometimes use the trailing arm to block and the lead arm to punch.

4. *Impact Drills*
[Corresponds to *Self-Defense*, Step 6, Drill 7]

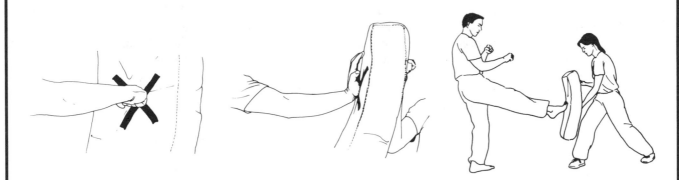

Group Management and Safety Tips

- Introduce impact drills only after students have developed correctly executed technique by practicing strikes in the air. This will help avoid jams and sprains that may result from impact against a bag with incorrect hand and foot positions.
- If using heavy bags, be sure that they are suspended from a secure wall or ceiling mount and have ample room to swing in all directions. For beginning-level students, bags weighing 25 to 50 pounds are most useful. Though relatively light and responsive, they have sufficient heft and weight to provide a challenge.
- If using hand-held shields, instruct shield holders in the safest, most effective way to present these training aids for striking. (Read manufacturer's instructions carefully: Most are held firmly by hand grips near the top and bottom of the concave side and

presented from a braced stance, with strikes being thrown toward the center of the convex surface.)
- Holders also may press the shield against a wall. If using this method, holders must be careful to grip the shield so that their hands are not on the exposed surface, where they might be struck.
- Try to have one bag (or shield) for every five students, so students do not stand around in long lines while awaiting their turn to strike or kick. If lines are unavoidable, have students stand far enough apart to allow them to practice their technique in the air while they wait.
- Explain to students that the purpose of impact drills is to develop precise targeting and biomechanical proficiency. Impact with a bag provides helpful (and occasionally painful) feedback on correct hand and foot position, trajectory, and targeting. It also

demonstrates the importance of balance, alignment, and movement from larger to smaller muscle groups in generating maximum force with minimum effort. "Muscling" a bag—using generally poor technique and relying instead on one's bulk and size—is inefficient and ineffective.

- Have students begin with very light impact and proceed gradually to 3/4 power and speed. Emphasize clear trajectories and precise points of contact. Warn students to avoid skidding on the bag's surface at impact, to minimize your having to treat skinned, bleeding knuckles. (If you think this might be a problem for some students, tape their knuckles with adhesive tape or have them wear leather gloves.)
- On each turn, students throw one strike or kick, stop the bag (if it is still moving after impact), and then go to the end of the line.
- After your students' initial efforts, tape large Xs on the bag or shield surface to challenge them to be even more precise in targeting. Tape Xs along the center axis of the bag or shield at varying heights to provide a number of smaller, more discrete targets.
- Do not allow students to practice those techniques where there is a high probability of jammed fingers (i.e., eye gouges and web strikes). The three front-facing techniques appropriate for impact drills are punches, palm-heel strikes, and front snap kicks.
- Ten repetitions of each technique on each limb is sufficient practice for your students' first efforts. Wrists and ankles may tire quickly during impact drills, increasing the likelihood of sprains or other injuries.

Equipment

- Heavy bag, weighing 25 to 50 pounds; 1 for every 5 students
- Hand-held shields (thick foam pads covered with canvas or tough plastic and measuring approximately 36" × 20" × 6")
- Masking tape
- Tennis or Ping-Pong balls (to increase difficulty)

Instructions and Cues to Class

- "Form lines of no more than five people in front of the bags (or shields). On your turn, position yourself in front of the bag as you

might be positioned relative to an attacker. From a balanced and solid stance, deliver a punch, palm-heel strike, or front snap kick to the area targeted on the bag (shield). Attend carefully to all aspects of the technique, including posture, hip rotation, trajectory, hand and foot position, striking surface, targeting, and retraction."
- "Your first few techniques should be very light. Gradually increase your speed and power to no more than 3/4 of your maximum capability. Do no more than 10 repetitions of each technique with each limb."

Student Option

- "Make your own training aid by stuffing a duffel or laundry bag with sawdust, sand, or old rags. Or wrap a large telephone book (several inches thick) with heavy duct or electrician's tape so that the entire surface is covered. Bore a hole about 2 inches from one end, draw a chain or heavy cord through the hole, and hang your training aid from a secure mount or beam."

Student Success Goals

- 20 punches to bag or shield (10 lead, 10 reverse punches)
- 20 palm-heel strikes to bag (10 lead, 10 trailing hand)
- 20 front snap kicks (10 lead, 10 trailing leg)

To Decrease Difficulty

- Use bags weighing 10 pounds or less.
- Use larger Xs for targeting.

To Increase Difficulty

- Use smaller Xs for more pinpoint targeting.
- Do a combination consisting of the same technique thrown twice in rapid succession to the same target.
- Repeat the preceding variation, but throw to two different targets (Xs).
- Throw combinations of different techniques to different targets.
- Let hanging bag swing and throw techniques to moving targets.
- Further challenge targeting skills by hanging tennis balls from the ceiling instead of bags. Then try Ping-Pong balls.

Step 7 Rear-Directed Counterattacks

In this step, your students will be mastering five counterattacks thrown toward an attacker standing directly behind them. These include

- elbow jabs,
- head butts,
- back kicks,
- shin scrapes, and
- heel stomps.

A surprise rear attack by an assailant whose face is obscured is particularly disconcerting and frightening to many. One way to help your students manage their fears about this kind of attack is to insure that they understand the counterattack options that are available to them when approached in this manner.

Begin by reminding your students that, as with any other direction of attack, they have six body weapons and a number of body targets available to them. Then, as you introduce each counterattack, encourage slow, careful practice until students' balance and body control are sufficient to allow them to take quicker, yet still precise, aim with hands and feet.

Keep in mind that balance and accuracy will likely be the primary challenges for your students in mastering these rear-directed techniques. Be prepared to provide feedback on posture and alignment. Stress that biomechanical proficiency will minimize any difficulties in maintaining balance. Also, frequently remind students to *look* where they are striking or kicking to improve accuracy. Beginning students are notorious for trying to do these techniques "blind," that is, while looking straight ahead rather than behind. Point out that in many cases they will be able to see the target located behind them. And even in those cases where students cannot see the targets, seeing other parts of the attacker's body will enable them to come fairly close to even small targets, such as the knee or solar plexus.

STUDENT KEYS TO SUCCESS

- Assume a wide, stable defensive stance.
- Demonstrate correct posture and alignment while setting up counterattacks (i.e., during the extension of the arm for elbow strikes or during the leg chamber for kicks).
- Maintain balance and body control throughout execution of the technique.
- Follow correct trajectories toward precise and appropriate targets and impacts with proper striking surfaces.
- Recover from strike delivery in a balanced, erect fashion and be prepared either to retreat or to throw additional counterattacks.

Rear-Directed Counterattacks Rating

BEGINNING LEVEL	SKILLED LEVEL
Elbow Jab	
• Maintains a high, narrow stance while executing elbow jabs • Pikes at the hip during elbow jab (Piking is done only during a kick/scrape/stomp series.) • Arcs into target instead of using straight-line trajectory • Looks straight ahead while executing elbow jab	• Assumes a wide, deep defensive stance in preparation for elbow jab • Keeps spine straight on all techniques, whether vertically aligned for elbow or piked for leg techniques • Executes a straight-line jab to the solar plexus or floating ribs • Looks in general direction of target, even if unable to see precise point of impact
Shin Scrape	
• Bends entire body forward instead of simply dropping chin to sight target • Is off-balance	• Impacts with heel or blade edge of foot • May pike slightly but keeps spine straight
Heel Stomp	
• Imprecise targeting	• Strikes heel to arch of attacker's foot
Head Butt	
• Attempts with an attacker who is too tall	• Determines that attacker's nose is accessible before using
Back Kick	
• Attempts to kick without piking (i.e., tries to maintain vertical alignment) • Spine rounded • Looks straight ahead • Chambers insufficiently so that heel arcs upward toward target • Misses targets • Loses balance easily	• Pikes slightly at hip while chambering kick • Spine straight • Trains eyes on target • Chambers leg high so that heel drives downward toward target • Launches kick along straight-line trajectory and impacts knee or shin with heel • Consistently maintains balance

Error Detection and Correction in Rear-Directed Counterattacks

Errors in these counterattacks—particularly those having to do with strike trajectory and striking surface—generally stem from incorrect posture, improper set-ups, and poor balance. Be sure that your students begin from a solid defensive stance, with a wide base of support and low center of gravity for throwing the elbow jab and head butt.

In preparation for the back kick, they will be raising their centers of gravity as they shift weight to one leg and chamber the other. As they pike slightly forward at the hip to line the striking foot up with the attacker's knee, be sure that they keep spines straight and look back in the general direction of the target. This should help them to maintain balance while extending the leg and to hit the relatively small target. Good balance through the scrape and stomp is helped by maintaining a straight spine (even when piking slightly forward at the hip) and a slight bend in the knee of the base (supporting) leg.

ERROR

CORRECTION

Elbow Jab

1. Defender's elbow jab trajectory is too short.

1. Have defender extend arm farther from trunk on set up. This gives the limb a longer distance to travel and build momentum.

2. Defender is using an arcing technique and brushing by targets.

2. Advise student to slip hips to the side and slightly rotate trunk to allow jab to move in a straight line toward the attacker's ribs or solar plexus. Emphasize that the correct striking surface is just above the elbow tip on the back of the defender's arm.

ERROR

CORRECTION

BACK KICK

1. Defender fails to chamber leg before kicking; foot goes directly from floor to target.

1. Explain to students the importance of the initial chamber in recruiting powerful extensor muscles for their kicks (a). Also point out that this lines the foot up for a straight-line drive through the target (b).

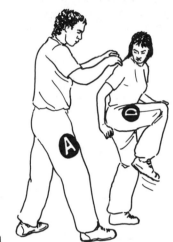

a

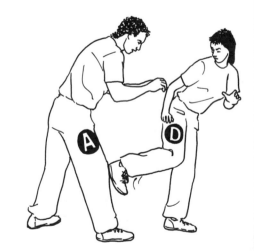

b

2. Defender's foot dangles loosely at the ankle during impact with target.

2. Have students keep the striking foot firmly flexed to avoid injuring the ankle on impact.

ERROR   **CORRECTION**

SCRAPE

1. Student scrapes down attacker's shin with ball of the foot.

1. Advise student that a more effective scraping surface is either the heel or the outside (blade) edge of the foot.

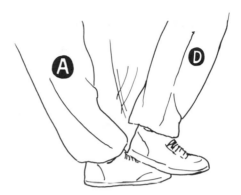

Stomp

1. Student uses the ball of the foot to deliver a stomp to the attacker's toes.

1. Remind student to keep the foot firmly flexed, while using the heel to stomp down on the attacker's arch—a quite fragile surface.

Rear-Directed Counterattack Drills

1. *Slow-Speed Solo Drill*
[Corresponds to *Self-Defense*, Step 7, Drill 1]

Group Management and Safety Tip

- Have students spread out around the training room, allowing at least 3 feet between one another to practice techniques.

Instructions and Cues to Class

- "The purpose of this drill is to give you an opportunity to practice throwing these techniques to imaginary targets and at your own pace. Move slowly and carefully, and pay close attention to such things as posture, alignment, set-ups, trajectories, and striking surfaces."

- "First, assume a low, wide defensive stance from which to throw elbow jabs. Be sure to set up the technique properly by extending your arm, palm up, away from your body at about a 45-degree angle. Slip your hips aside, slightly rotate your trunk as your eyes seek the target, and then move your elbow back along a straight-line trajectory toward imaginary ribs or solar plexus. Move slowly, monitoring all details of your technique."

- "Now do the same thing with back kicks only, and then the back kick-scrape-stomp combination. As you pike forward to line up your kicking foot with the imaginary target, keep your spine straight and your head turned in the direction you will be kicking. This will help to anchor your upper body as you extend your leg toward the target. As you slowly practice these leg techniques, work on balance and fluidity."

Student Option

- "Back kicks may be thrown to the attacker's shin, rather than the knee."

Student Success Goals

- 20 correctly executed elbow jabs (10 on each side)
- 20 correctly executed back kicks (10 on each side)
- 20 correctly executed back kick-scrape-stomp combinations (10 on each side)

To Decrease Difficulty

- If students have difficulty maintaining balance on kick or scrape, have them rest their hands on the back of a chair directly in front of them. After several repetitions have them grab the chair only when they lose balance. Later, remove the chair.

To Increase Difficulty

- Have students repeat the drill, this time with eyes closed to further improve balance and feel for the techniques.
- Have students increase speed to 3/4 of their top speed.

2. Targeting Drill With Partner
[Corresponds to *Self-Defense*, Step 7, Drill 2]

Group Management and Safety Tips

- Have each student select a partner. Then have one of each pair stand directly behind the other. The person standing behind will play the attacker, while the person standing in front with back turned toward his or her partner will play the defender. The attackers will not actually touch the defenders but should be close enough so that the defenders are within striking range.
- Advise the defenders to start slowly, and to stop at least 1 inch short of impacting on their partner's body with elbow jabs or head butts. Note that heel stomps should be off to the side of attacker's foot.

Instructions and Cues to Class

- "Defenders, stand directly in front of your partner-attacker. Direct combination attacks toward the appropriate targets on your partner's body, taking care to avoid making contact. Move slowly at first and concentrate on correct execution, accurate targeting, and good body control."

- "Use these combinations in this order:
  a) elbow jab-head butt combination
  b) back kick-scrape-stomp combination
  c) elbow jab-head butt-kick-scrape-stomp combination."

Student Option

- "If you have excellent balance and body control and if your partner-attacker agrees to this variation, very lightly impact the targets with appropriate slow-motion technique. You'll be using what we call 'whisper touch'—barely perceptible contact with your partner's body. This will give you a more realistic sense of range for using these techniques." (See Figure 7.1.)

Student Success Goals

- 20 correctly executed elbow jab-head butt combinations (10 on each side)
- 20 correctly executed back kick-scrape-stomp combinations (10 on each side)
- 10 correctly executed 5-technique combinations (5 on each side)

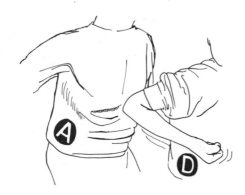

Figure 7.1 Student Option: The "whisper touch" involves barely perceptible contact with the partner's body.

Figure 7.2 To Decrease Difficulty: Have the attacker stand about 3 feet behind the defender.

To Decrease Difficulty

- Have defender practice only one technique at a time until he or she feels comfortable enough to try the suggested combinations.
- If the defender is concerned about striking a partner inadvertently, have the attacker stand about 3 feet behind the defender (see Figure 7.2). In this way, techniques will stop 12 to 24 inches short of targets. This should reassure both nervous defenders *and* nervous attackers.

To Increase Difficulty

- Have defenders increase speed of technique. Emphasize that techniques should not be thrown so fast that a defender risks losing control and inadvertently hitting a partner.

- Have defenders make up their own combinations of rear-directed counterattacks, using the five techniques introduced in this step. Suggest that they throw techniques in slow motion and that attackers move their heads toward the likely point of impact so defenders can determine which techniques might logically follow.

3. Impact Drills
[Corresponds to *Self-Defense*, Step 7, Drill 3]

Group Management and Safety Tips

- Impact drills should be introduced only after students have had an opportunity to develop correctly executed techniques by practicing strikes in the air.
- Use heavy bags or hand-held shields for practicing elbow jabs. Review the suggestions regarding size and weight of shields or bags that are offered in the section titled "Preparing Your Class for Success" (see page 3).

- The kick-scrape-stomp sequence can be practiced against a thick, regular tumbling mat propped on end against a wall. You may need to assign a couple of students to hold the mat on either side to keep it from sliding down the wall.
- Have students line up in front of impact devices. Aim for a ratio of five students at each device. Remind them to begin with very light impact and proceed gradually to about 3/4 of the maximum force they can generate.

- Have students first practice elbow jabs into hanging bags or shields. After each effort, a student should stop her or his bag and then move to the end of the line.
- After each student has thrown 20 elbow jabs (10 on each side), tape large Xs on the bag or shield. Have students aim for one of the Xs, without sacrificing speed or power.
- Next have students practice the kick-scrape-stomp sequence into the wall mat.
- After your students have thrown 20 of this combination (10 on each side) to a general area on the mat surface, have them throw back kicks only to one of the large Xs taped on the mat.
- These lines move pretty quickly so students have little time to stand around and get bored. Suggest that while awaiting their turns, they silently critique the performance of others in their line.

Equipment

- Heavy bag
- Hand-held shields
- Tumbling mat to stand on end
- Tape

Instructions and Cues to Class

- "Keep in mind that the reason for doing impact drills is to develop a feel for correct and effective technique. Actually impacting on a target provides important feedback regarding power and accuracy, as well as demonstrating how close we need to be to the attacker in order for these counterat-

tacks to be effective. For this reason we say that impact devices are excellent teachers."
- "Form lines of no more than five people in front of a bag (shield, mat). Stand within striking range, with your back to the device as you would be positioned in relation to an attacker approaching you from behind. Deliver elbow jabs (kick-scrape-stomp combinations) to the impact device, beginning with minimum force and working up to 3/4 of your maximum. When you have a feel for impacting on the target, work on improving your aim by first directing elbow jabs, and then back kicks to one of the large Xs taped on the bag (shield, mat)."

Student Options

- "Try different combinations of rear-directed counterattacks on the mat, such as elbow jab-stomp, scrape-stomp-elbow jab, elbow jab-kick, and so on."
- "To improve targeting of the scrape-stomp, tape a line on the mat between the X (imaginary knee) and the floor. Then tape another large X on the floor where the attacker's foot might be." (See Figure 7.3.)

Student Success Goals

- 20 elbow jabs into bag/shield (10 on each side)
- 20 kick-scrape-stomp sequences into cushioned wall surface (10 on each side)
- 18 to 20 elbow jabs impacting on an X
- 18 to 20 back kicks impacting on an X

Figure 7.3   Student Option: Tape Xs to improve targeting of the (a) kick- (b) scrape-stomp.

To Decrease Difficulty

- Allow more time for set-up (i.e., time for student to assume proper stance, gauge appropriate range, and sight target before executing technique).
- Use slow-speed techniques with minimal impact.
- Use larger Xs for targeting.

To Increase Difficulty

- Use smaller Xs for even more challenging targeting.
- Increase speed of techniques.

- Allow less time for set-up; require student to move rapidly into position and instantly execute techniques to pinpoint targets.
- Have student throw continuous techniques for 30 seconds. Emphasize speed and accuracy. Of the total number of counterattacks thrown, note the proportion that hit their targets (Xs). Have students work to increase either total number or proportion of accurate techniques or both. *Note:* Students awaiting their turns could count the total number of attacks and the number of hits that strike a designated target.

Step 8 **Side-Directed Counterattacks**

In this step, your students will be focusing on two counterattacks that can be used against an attacker approaching from the side. These two techniques are the hammerfist and the side stomp kick. Also introduced in this step is the side stance and side guard, which together make up the preparatory position for these two techniques.

Side-directed counterattacks enable a defender to respond immediately to an attack from either side of the body without first having to turn and face the assailant. By responding instantly from a side orientation, the defender not only saves time, but also minimizes exposure of the centerline.

The hammerfist is easily mastered by most students, although the side kick may present problems if a student lacks flexibility or loses balance easily. These problems are exacerbated if the student tries to throw the kick from an incorrect stance. Make sure that each student maintains a side orientation to the attacker from the initial chamber through the rechamber in order to prevent or at least minimize difficulties.

STUDENT KEYS TO SUCCESS

- Assume a wide-legged, stable side stance with arms in a side guard position.
- Execute a horizontal hammerfist, striking with little-finger-side of tightened fist to designated targets.
- Execute a side stomp kick by first lifting leg into chamber, then extending leg and foot along a straight line to impact with heel or blade edge of foot at designated target, and finally rechambering the leg.
- Maintain a side orientation throughout preparatory, execution, and follow-up phases of both techniques.
- Execute hammerfist and side kick in combination.

Side-Directed Counterattacks Rating

BEGINNING LEVEL	SKILLED LEVEL
Side Stance • Maintains high/narrow side stance • Holds guard in front of body rather than at the side	 • Maintains wide-legged, stable stance with side of body oriented toward attacker (see Figure 8.1) • Lead arm bends at 90 to 120 degrees and is held a few inches out from the side of the body; trailing arm cuts across trunk, so that fist is close to lead elbow (This places two fists between the defender's side and the attacker.)
Hammerfist • Arm fully extended throughout execution • Fist loose; wrist bent	 • Bent forearm moves from vertical to horizontal position and then straightens as fist is launched toward target • Fist tightens at impact; wrist line straight
Side Stomp Kick • Lacks clear chamber or rechamber in side stomp kick • Impacts on knee with toes or ball of foot • Drops guard when kicking • Lacks fluidity; kick appears choppy, awkward, off-balance	 • Moves fluidly from chamber through extension and back to rechamber • Impacts on target with blade edge or heel of foot • Maintains adequate side guard throughout kick • Movement fluid and unbroken; foot is in motion from leaving the floor through return after kick

Figure 8.1 The defender should maintain a side orientation to the attacker throughout the defense.

Error Detection and Correction in Side-Directed Counterattacks

First, check for errors in the side stance and side guard position. If this preparatory position is incorrect, execution of the hammerfist and the side stomp kick will be more difficult. Each technique consists of first positioning the striking agent (fist or foot) on the correct line of attack. A common error is to skip this initial positioning or to fudge it, which changes the trajectory of the technique. Finally, monitor fluidity and the ease with which students are able to move through these slightly more challenging techniques.

ERROR   **CORRECTION**

Side Stance

1. Defender assumes a high, narrow stance and turns centerline slightly toward attacker.

1. Have defender widen stance to about 1-1/2 shoulder-widths, bend knees slightly, tuck butt, and present the *side* of the body, while turning the head to look squarely at the attacker.

Hammerfist

1. Student impacts on target with arm fully extended and elbow locked.

1. Remind student to prepare for extension by dropping the lead fist forward until the arm, still bent at 90 degrees as in the guard position, is parallel to the ground. Although the arm straightens as the fist is launched toward the target, at impact there is still some flexion at the elbow. The defender's continued effort to straighten the arm after impact produces a more penetrating and powerful strike.

ERROR   **CORRECTION**

SIDE STOMP KICK

1. The defender swings a straightened leg up toward the target, then lets it drop back to the ground.

1. Remind student of the importance of the initial chamber in positioning the foot for a straight-line drive through the target and in providing a powerful hip thrust to launch the kick. The rechamber helps the defender maintain balance and sets up another kick.

2. Defender's foot dangles loosely at the ankle, and the toes lead on extension.

2. Have defender pull the top of his or her foot toward the shin so that the heel or blade edge of the foot leads on extension. Remind defender that a tight ankle at impact helps to avoid a sprain.

In General

1. Execution of these techniques is choppy and awkward.

1. Suggest to the student that she or he practice these techniques slowly and smoothly, without pause between the component parts, and gradually increase speed as fluidity increases.

Side-Directed Counterattack Drills

1. *Rocking Horse Acceleration Drill*
[Corresponds to *Self-Defense*, Step 8, Drills 1 and 2]

Group Management and Safety Tips

- Have students select partners and assume a side stance and guard in relation to one another. Both centerlines should be turned in the *same* direction, and students should be looking at one another.
- Remind students to stop short of full arm extension on hammerfists to avoid hyperextending their elbows.
- Side kicks should be thrown at less than full speed and 2 inches short of the targets to avoid injuries.

Instructions and Cues to Class

- "The purpose of this drill is to develop a feel for the hammerfist and side stomp kick, while gradually increasing speed to 3/4 of your maximum."
- "First assume a low, wide side stance and side guard in relation to your partner. Orient your centerlines in the same direction, while turning your heads to face one another."
- "Begin trading slow-speed hammerfists with your lead arms. One of you will be throwing right hammerfists, while the other will be using your left arm. When you are correctly executing the technique and placing your blows precisely 2 inches in front of their targets (e.g., nose, chin, jaw, temple, or throat), increase speed to 3/4 of your

maximum (or less, if you are uncertain about your ability to come to a screeching halt before impact)."
- "Once you both have thrown a minimum of 30 hammerfists on one side, turn and face the opposite direction and do 30 hammerfists using the other arm."
- "Repeat this drill with right and left side stomp kicks. Focus on accurate set-ups, clean and clear trajectories, precise targeting, quick retractions (rechambers), fluidity, and—eventually—speed."

Student Options

- "Another way to do these techniques is to orient your centerline in the opposite direction as your partner. The target is unchanged for the side stomp kick (side of partner's knee), although the base of the skull is now an additional target for the hammerfist."
- "When you are comfortable throwing single side-directed counterattacks, practice throwing combinations of these two techniques. First practice a hammerfist-side stomp kick combination, and then reverse order for a side stomp kick-hammerfist combination. Concentrate on interlocking technique in order to move smoothly and quickly from one technique to the other." [Corresponds to *Self-Defense*, Step 8, Drill 2]

Student Success Goals

120 single counterattacks
- 30 right hammerfists
- 30 left hammerfists
- 30 right side stomp kicks
- 30 left side stomp kicks

100 counterattack combinations
- 25 right hammerfist–side stomp kick combinations
- 25 left hammerfist–side stomp kick combinations
- 25 right side stomp kick–hammerfist combinations
- 25 left side stomp kick–hammerfist combinations

To Decrease Difficulty

- Have students maintain slow speed.
- Suggest that partners increase distance between themselves if they are concerned about being able to stop short of striking each other.
- If students are having a difficult time learning one of these counterattacks, break the technique down into component parts consisting of first a set-up (i.e., positioning the fist or foot on the line of attack), followed by extension, and then retraction (rechamber). When all of these elements are mastered, have students put them together in one fluid movement.

To Increase Difficulty

- Have students take turns throwing as many hammerfists as they can in 15 seconds. On each of their turns, have them try to increase the number of correctly executed hammerfists thrown within the time allotted. (For safety's sake, remind them to stop short of full elbow extension.)
- Repeat with side stomp kicks.
- Have skilled students trade rapid single and combination side-directed counterattacks of their choice. Have them kiyai on the single techniques or on the last technique of a combination to signal that their partners may now attack them.
- Have skilled students experiment with inside and outside blocks thrown from a side stance to deflect an incoming hammerfist (see Figure 8.2). Note that when partners' centerlines are oriented in the same direction, the inside block is used; when partners' centerlines are oriented in the opposite direction, the outside block is used.

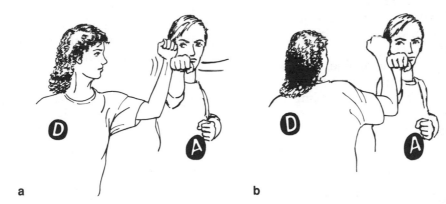

a   b

Figure 8.2 To Increase Difficulty: Have students use (a) inside blocks or (b) outside blocks to deflect hammerfists.

2. *Impact Drills*

[Corresponds to *Self-Defense*, Step 8, Drill 3]

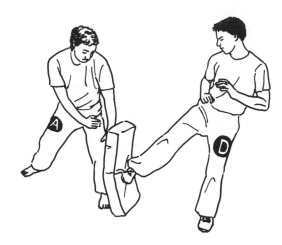

Group Management and Safety Tips

- Introduce impact drills only after students have had an opportunity to develop correctly executed techniques in nonimpact partner drills.
- The ideal equipment for practicing these two side-directed counterattacks is a long, free-hanging heavy bag hung so that the lowest point is no more than 16 inches from the floor. This allows defenders to throw a hammerfist to the side of the bag and a side stomp kick to the front surface. Because this long bag offers both planes of action, it is most useful for practicing combinations of these two techniques.
- If a heavy bag is not available, these techniques can be practiced singly against shields, smaller bags, or tumbling mats standing on end.
- Remind students that the purpose of impact drills is to get a feel for biomechanically correct technique: good balance, proper stance, correct trajectories, appropriate striking surfaces of the hand and foot, and precise targeting.
- Have students line up in front of impact devices, five students to each device. Caution them to begin with very light impact, increasing to greater force only when they have a sense of how much "give" there is in the device.
- First, have students practice hammerfists. Have them assume a side stance and orient themselves in such a way so as to allow the hammerfist to move along a curved-line, horizontal trajectory to hit the target. If working with a free-hanging bag, they will be positioned at a right angle to the bag, in much the way they worked with partners. If using a shield or mat held against a wall, they will need to stand with their backs to the wall in order to strike the target at a correct angle.
- Next have students practice side stomp kicks against whichever device is being used. Emphasize the use of the blade edge or heel of the foot for striking and the importance of quick, complete rechambers of the kicking leg.
- Let the person who has just completed the impact drill hold the bag/mat/shield for the next person in line.

Equipment

- Heavy bag (or, if heavy bags are unavailable, hand-held shields, smaller bags, and tumbling mats standing on end)
- Tape (to decrease/increase difficulty)

Instructions and Cues to Class

- "Form lines of no more than five people in front of each impact device. Orient yourself toward the device in such a way so as to be able to correctly execute the technique and impact the bag (shield, mat). On your first turn, strike or kick lightly. With each turn, increase force until you reach 3/4 of your maximum power. Use less force if there is little 'give' in the device, such as in a thin mat propped against a wall. Do five counterattacks each turn, and then move quickly to hold the impact device for the next person in line."

Student Option

- "Practice single techniques first, and then do combinations. If you have a long, heavy bag, you will be able to do combinations without having to reposition yourself. If you are using a shield or mat held against the wall, you'll be doing a hammerfist with your back to the wall and a side stomp kick at a right angle to the wall. This will require that you reposition yourself between each technique of your combination or throw one of them in the air."

Student Success Goals

- 10 right hammerfists
- 10 left hammerfists
- 10 right side stomp kicks
- 10 left side stomp kicks

To Decrease Difficulty

- Allow extra time for the student to assume proper stance relative to the device, to gauge appropriate range, and to sight target before launching technique or counterattack.

- Encourage slow-speed technique with minimal force of impact. Emphasize precise targeting and use of correct striking surface.
- Use tape to make very large Xs for targeting.

To Increase Difficulty

- Use smaller Xs for precision targeting.
- Allow less time for set-up; require skilled students to move more rapidly into position and immediately execute counterattacks to pinpoint targets.
- Have skilled students throw continuous counterattacks (hammerfist or side stomp kick) for 60 seconds or until they miss the X three times. Count the number of precisely targeted and well executed counterattacks.

Step 9 Response to Attempted Front Choke Hold

From this point forward, you'll be helping your students explore the application of foundation skills (i.e., evasions, blocks, and counterattacks) to a number of common grab attacks. A grab attack involves the seizing of another person or a part of his or her body, such as the wrist, arm, throat, or hair.

In this step, your students will be learning the flying wedge and push-away, a response to an *attempted* front choke hold. By deflecting the attacker's arms to the sides and immediately pushing him or her backwards, the defender prevents the assailant from reaching the throat and securing a stranglehold—a dangerous and life-threatening attack. In the next step, your students will build on this response as they learn how to defend against a *secured* front choke hold, that is, one in which the attacker has actually managed to grasp the defender by the throat.

Practice of the flying wedge and push-away will give your students further opportunity to develop and hone a sense of timing and range, central elements in this and every other defense.

STUDENT KEYS TO SUCCESS

- Assume a solid, braced defensive stance in preparation for defense against a grab attack.
- Move vertical forearms explosively to either side, intercept the attacker's arms, wrist-to-wrist, and deflect them out to the sides.
- Instantly place palm heels on the attacker's chest, step forward, and shove the attacker backward.
- Sharpen the sense of range and timing, which enables one to adapt one's response to attackers of different size, strength, reach, and speed.

Response to an Attempted Front Choke Hold Rating

BEGINNING LEVEL	SKILLED LEVEL
• Assumes a high, narrow defensive stance • Responds too late to intercept and prevent grab	• Assumes a wide, low, braced stance • Responds in timely manner, intercepting attacker before she or he is able to grab throat
• Intercepts at elbows or upper arm; strikes with back of wrist rather than ulnar edge	• Executes a technically correct flying wedge—moves from palm-in to palm-out position, intercepts wrist-to-wrist and at a right angle to attacker's arms, impacts with ulnar edge of wrist (see Figure 9.1)
• Executes a weak, ineffective push-away; fails to create distance between attacker and self	• Executes a powerful, effective push-away by maintaining erect posture, keeping eyes straight ahead, correctly placing palm heels on attacker's chest, and straightening elbows while stepping and pushing (see Figure 9.2)
• Does a faint, demoralized kiyai	• Does a loud kiyai to startle an attacker and empower him- or herself.

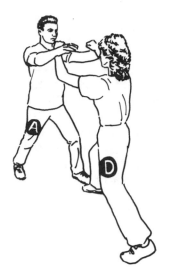

Figure 9.1   A correctly executed flying wedge.

Figure 9.2   In a correctly executed push-away, the defender places palm heels on the attacker's chest, then straightens elbows while pushing away.

Error Detection and Correction in a Flying Wedge and Push-Away

Look for errors related to the timing of the technique, most often having to do with not responding quickly enough to prevent a hold from being secured. Also watch for errors in stance and posture during *both* the flying wedge and the push-away. Monitor details such as point of interception, striking surface, rotation of forearms, placement of palm heels, angle at elbow, and so on. There is considerable detail to be attended to in this seemingly "simple" defense.

ERROR

CORRECTION

ERROR	CORRECTION
1. Defender fails to prevent choke hold from being secured.	1. Defender is responding too late. Advise student to note an attacker's intention to grab as early as possible (by monitoring his or her eyes, movement of shoulders and hands, or even more subtle behavioral cues, such as changes in body tension, shifts in weight, etc.) and to begin the flying wedge the instant the attack is signaled.

ERROR

CORRECTION

2. Student interrupts grab at attacker's elbows or upper arms.

2. Advise student to concentrate on intercepting at attacker's wrists, using ulnar edge of his or her own wrists as the striking surface. Point out that intercepting at the attacker's elbows will not prevent the choke hold from being secured, because the attacker can still bend his or her arm to reach the defender's throat.

3. Defender executes timely wedge but lacks the strength to hold the attacker's hands away from the throat for long.

3. Advise defender to maximize holding power by holding his or her elbow at 90 to 120 degrees of flexion. Also, encourage defender to minimize the pause between the wedge and push-away.

4. Defender is not able to create much distance between self and attacker with the push-away.

4. First, have defender check details of posture and stance that allow a strong shove:
   - Is the back straight, and does he or she step forward with the lead leg while shoving?
   - Are eyes trained straight ahead on the push, or does the head drop forward? Are the elbows bent at 90 to 120 degrees on impact with the chest to insure some pushing power?
   - Are palm heels placed on the firm, muscular surface just below the collarbone and above the breasts?

   Attention to these details generally enables even a much smaller and lighter person to unbalance a bigger attacker.

Flying Wedge and Push-Away Drills

1. Mirror Drill
[Corresponds to *Self-Defense*, Step 9, Drill 1]

Group Management and Safety Tips

- Have students stand in front of a large, full-length mirror and assume correct defensive stances.
- Have them practice flying wedges, starting slowly and then increasing to 3/4 maximum speed. Once students are correctly executing flying wedges, have them add kiyais.
- Make sure each student has sufficient space to throw large, powerful flying wedges while monitoring the details of their technique in the mirror.

Equipment

- Full-length mirrors
- Large book to drop (to increase difficulty)

Instructions and Cues to Class

- "Assume a wide, low defensive stance in front of the mirror. Begin throwing slow-speed flying wedges, and attend to all aspects of the technique. Think of deflecting an attacker's arms—not just with *your* arms, but rather with your entire body. Think of pushing with your legs as you execute the wedge. Gradually increase speed to 3/4 of your maximum. Add kiyais to the last 10 repetitions."

Student Option

- "Try closing your eyes on a few repetitions to get a better feel for the technique."

Student Success Goals

- 15 repetitions of a correctly executed flying wedge without a kiyai
- 10 repetitions of a correctly executed flying wedge with a kiyai

To Decrease Difficulty

- Drill is already in simplest form.

To Increase Difficulty

- Increase the number and speed of flying wedges.
- Stand in front of students with a large object, such as a book, held high. Instruct students to begin the flying wedge the instant they see you drop the item and to complete it before the object hits the ground. The item dropped must be heavy enough to make a resounding noise when it hits. This is a quick and enjoyable drill for increasing speed of technique, once students have mastered the mechanics of the move.

2. Progressive Partner Drill
[Corresponds to *Self-Defense*, Step 9, Drill 2]

Group Management and Safety Tips

- Have each student select a partner. Then have the entire group form two parallel lines with partners facing one another in defensive stances and at a distance of about 1 arm's-length (i.e., inside the critical distance zone).
- Advise attackers to keep their fingers together and thumbs tucked (to avoid accidental sprains and jams) and their arms apart as they reach.
- Emphasize that the push-away should be *very* light to minimize the possibility of someone being shoved to the floor and incurring injury.

- Have both attackers and defenders move only as fast as they are able to while maintaining good control and correct form.

Instructions and Cues to Class

- "Now you'll have an opportunity to sharpen your sense of range and timing, as you practice this defense with a partner. First, assume defensive stances, facing one another, and prepare to move through the five stages of this drill."
- "In the first stage, you'll nod to your partner to indicate your readiness to be attacked. In response to a series of 25 attempted front choke holds, throw solid, correctly executed flying wedges."
- "In the second stage, respond to 20 attempted front choke holds with a flying wedge plus a push-away."
- "On the next set of 15 attacks and defenses, add kiyais to both the wedge and the push-away."
- "In the fourth stage, the attackers will add loud, angry-sounding shouts as they reach for the defenders' throats, trying to rattle defenders and distract their focus from their defense. Do this 10 times."
- "Finally, in the last stage, the attacker will decide when to attack. Defenders will respond in a spirited manner with correctly executed and well-timed technique. Practice this five times."

Student Success Goals

- 25 flying wedges only
- 20 flying wedges plus push-aways
- 15 repetitions of entire sequence with kiyais
- 10 repetitions with attacker shouting
- 5 repetitions with attacker deciding when to grab

Student Option

- "When you've completed the drill, try stepping on the attacker's foot as you do the push-away. Don't actually shove your partner as you do this unbalancing technique. Instead, lightly place your hands on the chest while stepping with considerably *less* than full weight on your partner's foot. Try to get a sense of this variation without actually causing your practice partner to lose balance and fall." (See Figure 9.3.)

Figure 9.3 Student Option: Step on attacker's foot as you push away.

To Decrease Difficulty

- Have attackers grab more slowly, so that defenders have more time to note incoming attack and respond effectively. Draw defender's attention to cues that signal an attacker's intent to grab. Do more repetitions at each stage, before moving on to the next.
- Have defenders practice the wedge followed by the push-away without partners, until the entire sequence is fluid and correct. Then have them try again with a partner.

To Increase Difficulty

- Have attackers increase speed of attack. To challenge defender's ability to monitor and predict an attack, advise attackers to avoid telegraphing their intention to defenders before grabbing. Suggest that attacks in the fifth stage of this drill be sudden and explosive.
- A challenging variation on this drill is to form teams of three people to play a sort of "monkey-in-the-middle." The two people on either side of the middle person will alternate front choke attempts. The middle person will defend against first one, then the other, then the first again, and so on. Attackers can grab as soon as the defender turns back toward them and *makes eye contact*. Defenders must quickly adjust to the slightly different timing, size, strength, and limb length of the two attackers in this drill of constantly shifting ranges.

3. Milling With Flying Wedge

[Corresponds to *Self-Defense*, Step 9, Drill 3]

Group Management and Safety Tips

- Have four or more students mill rapidly about a good-sized room, trying to maintain awareness of everyone else. Participants should be especially conscious of others passing within their critical distance zones.
- Be sure that there is sufficient space to allow pretty energetic milling without risk of colliding with others.
- Instruct students to respond to attempted front choke holds with the flying wedge *only*. Inclusion of a push-away in this drill could result in an attacker being inadvertently shoved into a third person milling nearby.
- Remind attackers to keep their fingers together and thumbs tucked as they grab, in order to avoid jams or sprains.
- Encourage students to stay focused and calm despite the unpredictable and spontaneous nature of this drill and the rapid and energetic movement it calls for.

Instructions and Cues to Class

- "Mill rapidly about the room, noting anyone who passes within your CDZ. From time to time, select someone to attack. Point and loudly shout, 'You!' When he or she pauses and makes eye contact with you, attempt a front choke hold."
- "If someone points to you and shouts, 'You!,' prepare to execute a flying wedge in response to an attempted front choke. Intercept the attack, and then begin to mill again until you are once more called to defend yourself or until you decide to attack."

Student Option

- "Note the range from which the attacker comes at you. If the attack is initiated from outside the critical distance zone, respond with an evasive sidestep. If the attack is launched from within the CDZ, respond with a flying wedge. This helps you practice the skills of perceiving range of attacks and responding appropriately."

Student Success Goal

- 2 minutes of milling, playing both attacker and defender roles

To Decrease Difficulty

- Slow the pace of the drill by having students walk about the room rather than mill rapidly.
- Suggest to attackers that they pause for a few seconds longer between shouting "You!" and launching their attack, so that defenders have plenty of time to set up for their defense. Gradually increase the speed of attack.

To Increase Difficulty

- Increase the pace of the drill.
- Have attackers shout "You!" and then launch the attack the instant eye contact is made with targeted defender.
- Dim the lights and do this drill in semi-darkness. You may need to have students slow down a bit at first, and then gradually increase speed during this drill variation.

Step 10 Response to Secured Front Choke Hold

In this step, your students will be building on the skills learned in the previous step as they learn how to respond to a secured front choke hold—one in which the attacker has been able to grasp the defender in a life-threatening front choke hold. A response to this dangerous and frightening form of attack requires that the defender first distract the attacker with a sharp kick to the knee or shin, follow with a flying wedge to break the attacker's grip on the defender's throat, and finish with a palm-heel strike to the nose. Notice that the defense incorporates the flying wedge, taught in the previous step, as well as two of the front-facing strikes learned in Step 6.

Given the life-threatening nature of this attack, your students may exhibit more nervousness than with other less intrusive or potentially deadly grabs. Take your time in working through the first drill, "Building the Technique Drill." Invite your students to focus on the details of

each move, rather than on any discomfort they might be experiencing. Make sure that each component is fully mastered before adding the next. This will help your students build smooth and rapid transitions between each of the component parts of this defense.

STUDENT KEYS TO SUCCESS

- Assume a solid, braced defensive stance in preparation for attack.
- When grabbed by the throat, grab the attacker's wrists firmly, execute a front snap kick to the knee or shin, follow with the flying wedge to break the hold, and finish with a palm-heel strike to the nose.
- Move in rapid succession from one move to another in a balanced, fluid manner.
- Maintain a calm and focused state of mind throughout the execution of this defense.

Response to a Secured Front Choke Hold Rating

BEGINNING LEVEL	SKILLED LEVEL
• Forgets to grab hold of attacker's wrists to maintain balance during front snap kick • Lacks initial chamber or rechamber • Kicks too high, far from target • Places kicking foot right next to base foot so that stance for throwing flying wedge is high and narrow, or attempts wedge while leg is still in rechamber position • Uses arms only for executing wedge • Drops nonstriking arm during execution of palm-heel strike • Lacks penetration, striking target when elbow is already fully extended • Forgets to shout kiyai or speaks, rather than shouts, kiyai.	• Grasps attacker's wrists firmly in preparation for powerful, balanced front snap kick • Chambers before and after extension of leg • Places ball of foot a few inches to the side of partner's knee or shin (see Figure 10.1) • Rechambers kicking leg rapidly, and assumes wide, low stance for flying wedge • Draws power from legs and trunk in executing wedge • Maintains centerline coverage with nonstriking arm throughout execution of palm-heel strike • Strikes imaginary target (2 inches in front of partner's nose) while striking arm is still bent so that continued extension would result in even greater penetration • Incorporates loud and startling kiyais on all three moves

Figure 10.1   To avoid injury, have students kick to an imaginary target to the side of the partner's knee.

Error Detection and Correction in a Secured Front Choke Hold

Each technique in this response must be done correctly in order to set up for the next. A powerful and well-aimed front snap kick will cause the assailant to pike forward and loosen his grip. A correctly executed flying wedge completes the break and opens up the attacker's centerline for a palm-heel strike to the nose.

Make sure your students give each technique full attention to insure that it is done correctly and powerfully. A common tendency is to rush through this sequence, which results in loss of balance, weak technique, and missed targets. While encouraging your students to give each technique its due, also have them work on moving fluidly and in a balanced manner from one move to the next. The response should be "of a piece," with students moving easily and rapidly through the transitions between techniques.

ERROR

CORRECTION

1. Your student's kick is missing the target.

2. Student is stepping down from the kick into a high, narrow stance.

3. Your student is forgetting to drop the foot to the ground following the kick and is attempting to throw the wedge from a one-legged stance.

1. To improve accuracy, have your student glance at the target an instant before launching the kick.

2. This is not the most effective stance from which to throw the flying wedge. Suggest that your student widen and deepen the stance by placing feet 1-1/2 shoulder-widths apart, bending the knees, and lowering the center of gravity.

3. Advise your student that wedges are most effective when thrown from a solid, wide, stable stance as opposed to a one-legged "crane" stance.

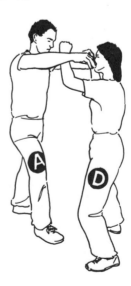

ERROR	CORRECTION
4. Student's guard drops following the wedge.	4. Have your student concentrate on rapidly returning to a protective guard the instant the wedge is completed. This protects the centerline from possible strikes and sets the student up to make strikes. It also positions arms and hands for another flying wedge in the event that the assailant tries to resecure the front choke hold.
5. Student is missing targets (knee/shin and nose) or impact points (assailant's wrists).	5. Advise your student to not rush through this response, but rather to take it one technique at a time. Doing a loud kiyai on each technique will help in correctly pacing through the response.

Response to Secured Front Choke Hold Drills

1. *Building the Technique Drill*
[Corresponds to *Self-Defense*, Step 10, Drill 1]

Group Management and Safety Tips

- Have each student select a partner. Then have the entire group form two parallel lines with partners facing one another in defensive stances and from a distance of about 1 arm's-length (i.e., inside the critical distance zone).
- Make sure that students have sufficient room to perform this response without risk of striking or being struck by pairs on either side of them (there should be at least 4 feet between pairs).
- Make sure students understand that when they grab their partners during these drills, they must place their hands high on the *shoulders* rather than on the neck or throat in order to avoid rendering a partner unconscious. Suggest that they grab fairly firmly.
- All front snap kicks should be aimed at imaginary targets to the side of partner's knees or shins to avoid injury to person playing attacker.
- Palm-heel strikes should be "pulled" (i.e., stopped 2 inches short of partner's nose). Defenders should build speed only to the point where they are still able to maintain control of the technique.
- Use your voice (and a loud, concise count) to pace students. Allow sufficient time for students to concentrate on details of correct execution for each component part. However, don't count so slowly that students lose a sense of flow and continuity from one move to the next.

Instructions and Cues to Class

- "Assume a defensive stance facing your practice partner. You'll be building this response one technique at a time. On count '1,' the attacker will grab the defender high on the shoulders. The defender will respond by firmly grabbing the attacker's wrists. This action startles the attacker and stabilizes the defender in preparation for a front snap kick. On count '2,' the defender throws this kick to an imaginary target outside the attacker's knees or shins. Then the defender steps down into a wide, stable stance. We'll be repeating this combination approximately 15 times or until your kicks are correctly executed."

- "Now we'll add a count of '3,' and defenders will execute a flying wedge to break the choke hold. Again, do a number of these until you are moving easily and fluidly from kick to wedge. We'll repeat this 15 times."
- "On count '4,' defenders add a palm-heel strike to the nose. As before, do approximately 15 repetitions, on my cue."
- "Finally, on the defender's nod, the attacker will grab. Defenders should respond with the entire sequence in a smooth, continuous flow that does not sacrifice accuracy or power. Defenders, be sure to kiyai on each technique."

Student Options

- N/A

Student Success Goals

- 15 repetitions of first two counts, by the count
- 15 repetitions of first three counts, by the count
- 15 repetitions of all four counts, by the count
- 15 repetitions of entire sequence, with kiyais

To Decrease Difficulty

- As you build the response, do a greater number of repetitions at each count. Count slowly enough to allow students to properly set up for each technique. When students are ready to do the entire sequence in a smooth, continuous fashion, have them move at half speed and only gradually work up to full speed. Be sure that the response is mastered before adding any of the stressors described in Drill 2.

To Increase Difficulty

- When students have mastered the entire sequence, have them quickly change partners. This can be done by having the attackers move down one person to their right. Do this every two or three repetitions, so that defenders are required to adjust to differences between attackers.

2. Adding Stressors Drill
[Corresponds to *Self-Defense*, Step 10, Drill 2]

Group Management and Safety Tips

- Same as for Drill 1

Instructions and Cues to Class

- "To give defenders an opportunity to develop skill in moving past panic or momentary disorientation, attackers can shout 'Shut up!' or 'Don't move!' when they grab. This stressor, as well as those following, enables defenders to practice recovering quickly from a startled response and moving into a deliberate and effective defense. Do 10 repetitions with attackers shouting."

- "Now try at least 10 repetitions in which the attacker decides when to attack. Attackers should be sure to pause between each interaction to allow defender to center and refocus."
- "In this last set of 10 repetitions, defenders will assume the preparatory position with eyes closed. Attackers, attack when you are ready. Defenders, be sure to open your eyes instantly upon being grabbed, take stock of the situation, and move very deliberately and in a controlled fashion to effect a release. Note whether your startled response lessens with each repetition."

Student Options

- N/A

Student Success Goals

- 10 repetitions with attacker shouting on grab
- 10 repetitions with attacker choosing when to attack
- 10 repetitions of attacks initiated with defender's eyes closed

To Decrease Difficulty

- Increase the number of repetitions for each stressor.
- Advise students to slow down attacks and defenses.

To Increase Difficulty

- During the portion of this drill that begins with defenders' eyes closed, have attackers quickly and silently change partners so that defenders will not know *who* is grabbing them until they are grabbed and have opened their eyes. (Give visual cues to attackers so that they all switch partners and then attack in unison.) Not knowing when they will be grabbed or by whom increases the defenders' startled response and also requires that they quickly adjust for changes in limb length and height of their attackers in implementing the defense.

3. Variable Strike Drill

[Corresponds to *Self-Defense*, Step 10, Drill 3]

Group Management and Safety Tips

- Same as for Drill 1

Instructions and Cues to Class

- "This drill is designed to help you develop greater flexibility of response and skill in building sequences of moves. Each defense will begin with the front snap kick followed by the flying wedge. Rather than finishing with the palm-heel strike, however, you'll be substituting other front-facing strikes."
- "Begin with eye gouges, then try web strikes, punches, and then push-aways. Do 10 repetitions with each of the substitute strikes or the push-away."
- "Finally, do 10 repetitions using whichever of these five techniques (palm-heel, web strike, punch, eye gouge, and push-away) you wish as the third technique in this response."

Student Success Goals

- 10 repetitions of sequence, substituting eye gouges for palm-heel strikes
- 10 repetitions of sequence, substituting web strikes for palm-heel strikes
- 10 repetitions of sequence, substituting a punch to the nose, chin, or throat for the palm-heel strike
- 10 repetitions of sequence, finishing with the push-away rather than a strike
- 10 repetitions of the sequence, using any of the above as the final technique

Student Options

- N/A

To Decrease Difficulty

- Do additional repetitions at a slower pace.

To Increase Difficulty

- Have students do the standard response (e.g., kick, wedge, palm-heel) and then add a fourth technique (e.g., another of the front-facing strikes or a push-away). This variation helps students learn how to build even longer combinations.
- Attackers can respond as if each strike had landed by moving their heads "toward the pain."
- When defenders are proficient in throwing a sequence of four techniques, have them try five, then six, and so on. Remind them to pause momentarily between techniques to determine "impact" and to exercise good control at all times in order to avoid actually striking a partner.

Step 11 Response to Mugger's Hold

In this step and the next, your students will be learning responses to grab attacks coming from behind them. The first of these attacks, called a mugger's hold, involves an assailant wrapping his or her forearm around the defender's neck and throat and applying pressure. The assailant uses the free hand to suppress a scream or to grab the defender's arm or hair. In a variation on this grab, the assailant uses the free hand to grip the wrist of the arm wrapped across the defender's throat (see Figure 11.1). This secured hold places even greater pressure on the defender's throat and is more difficult to dislodge.

The response to a mugger's hold consists of first relieving the pressure on the throat by rolling the attacker's arm down the chest while tucking the chin. The defender then instantly follows up with rear-directed counterattacks, such as the elbow jab and back kick. This defense is used in response to both versions of the mugger's hold, although the secured hold is decidedly more difficult to break.

STUDENT KEYS TO SUCCESS

- Assume a wide, low, braced defensive stance in preparation for effecting a release.
- Raise both elbows high and roll the attacker's arm downward to pin against chest in a palm-out position
- Tuck chin and execute a powerful elbow jab to the solar plexus or ribs followed by an accurately placed back kick to knee or shin.
- Move fluidly and in a balanced manner from one component of this defense to the next.

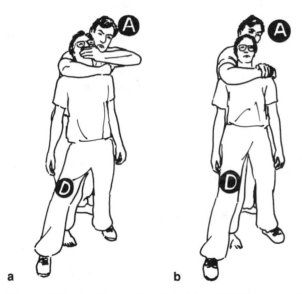

a   b

Figure 11.1 (a) The mugger's hold and (b) the secured mugger's hold.

Response to Mugger's Hold Rating

BEGINNING LEVEL	SKILLED LEVEL
• Maintains high narrow stance, even after having been grabbed • Pikes forward when grabbed from behind	• Lowers center of gravity, and widens base of support of defensive stance • Maintains vertical posture and prevents being toppled forward by aligning long line of stance with the force from behind
• Grabs assailant's hands/arm tentatively	• Grabs assailant's hands/arm forcefully, using as much of own hand and wrist as possible
• Fails to raise elbows, resulting in use of wrists only for roll-down • Forgets/delays chin tuck	• Raises elbows in order to recruit powerful trunk muscles for roll-down (see Figure 11.2) • Immediately and consistently tucks chin when assailant's arm is removed
• Sets up elbow on side of body where there are fewer accessible targets • Fails to set up elbow, resulting in fuzzy trajectory and weak technique • Barely chambers kick, scoops foot in an upward arc to target, and fails to rechamber	• Judges correctly the side of assailant's body that presents more accessible targets • Sets up elbow to allow for a long, clear, straight-line thrust to target (see Figure 11.3) • Chambers kicking leg, drives straight down and through target, and rechambers leg before setting it down
• Forgets to "sight" target for elbow jab or kick • Bends forward at waist when kicking, resulting in loss of balance	• Looks in direction of targets to improve aim • Pikes slightly forward at hips while maintaining an erect spine in order to maximize penetration of kick and still maintain balance
• Does pattern by rote, does not adapt or modify response as required by circumstances	• Adapts response to changing situation (i.e., adds other kicks and strikes in different combinations)

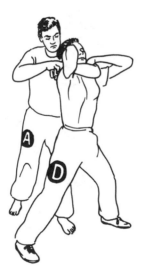

Figure 11.2 Raise elbows to recruit trunk muscles for roll-down.

Figure 11.3 Set up elbow for straight-line run to target.

Error Detection and Correction in Response to Mugger's Hold

Common errors in this response are most often caused by poor balance, incorrect posture and stance, and sloppy set-ups for counterattacks. Some of these are detailed here. Additional common errors associated with simple elbow jabs and back kicks are outlined in *Self-Defense*, Step 7.

ERROR

CORRECTION

1. Your student is unable to remove the assailant's arm from his or her throat.

2. Student is bending forward from the waist as she or he tucks chin.

3. Student is easily knocked off balance when grabbed.

1. Make sure that your student is lifting his or her elbows *before* attempting the roll-down. This recruits more powerful trunk muscles for the release, so that a defender isn't opposing an attacker's arm and chest muscles with only the strength in his or her fingers and wrists. If your student is *still* unable to break the hold after first lifting the elbows, suggest going to immediate counterattack.

2. Advise student that in this position she or he is likely to lose balance and pitch forward. Suggest that the spine be kept perpendicular to the floor.

3. Make sure the student has one leg forward to brace him- or herself against a shove forward. Suggest deepening the stance by bending knees and broadening (lengthening) base of support.

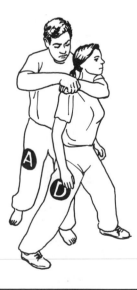

ERROR	**CORRECTION**
4. Student consistently misses targets.	4. Frequently a student will attempt to do a "blind" technique by keeping eyes forward while throwing rear-directed counterattacks. The student should look in the general direction of the target, even if she or he cannot actually see the attacker's ribs/solar plexus/knees/shins. Note whether using the opposite leg and arm would result in easier access and sighting of appropriate targets.
5. Student's jabs or kicks lack power.	5. Make sure the student is taking time to set up the elbow jab and kick. Proper preparatory position, straight-line trajectories, and correct range will increase power and effectiveness of these techniques.

Response to Mugger's Hold Drills

1. *Building the Technique Drill*
[Corresponds to *Self-Defense*, Step 11, Drill 1]

Group Management and Safety Tips

- Have each student select a partner. Then have the entire group form two parallel lines, both facing out in the same direction. Designate those standing in front as defenders and have them assume a defensive stance. Students in the back row should stand directly behind their partners.
- Make sure that students have sufficient room to perform this response without risk of striking or being struck by students on either side of them.
- Instruct students playing attacker to grab at the level of the defender's Adam's apple and with only light pressure.
- Instruct students to stop 1 inch short of impacting on partner's ribs or solar plexus when executing the elbow jab.
- Remind students to kick to imaginary targets about 6 inches to the side of their partners' knees or shins.

Instructions and Cues to Class

- "Defenders, assume a defensive stance directly in front of your partners. You'll be building this response, one move at a time. On the count of '1,' the attacker will grab you in an unsecured mugger's hold."
- "On the count of '2,' you will grab the attacker's forearm just below the elbow and at the juncture of the wrist and hand, and roll it *down* and *into* your chest. As soon as the attacker's forearm is off your throat, tuck your chin to prevent the attacker from reestablishing the hold. We'll be doing 10 repetitions of the first 2 counts."
- "On the count of '3,' defenders will set up an elbow jab. Do this by extending your arm in a palm-up position and lining it up with the target."
- "On count '4,' release the elbow jab. Stop short of actually impacting on your partner's ribs or solar plexus. Be prepared to do 10 repetitions of the first four counts."

partner's ribs or solar plexus. Be prepared to do 10 repetitions of the first four counts."

- "On the count of '5,' defenders will chamber the kicking leg."
- "And on '6,' throw a back kick to an imaginary target a few inches to the outside of the attacker's knee or shin. Be sure to rechamber the leg before stepping down. Prepare to repeat the first six counts a minimum of 10 times."
- "Now that you have practiced the entire sequence by my count, move through the entire response smoothly and fluidly on your own. Defenders will cue attackers to attack by shouting 'Now!' In response to the grab, defenders will execute the entire response, adding kiyais to both the jab and kick. Do 10 repetitions on your own."
- "Next, the defenders will become the attackers and vice versa. After that we'll repeat the entire sequence with attackers using a secured mugger's hold."

Student Options

- N/A

Student Success Goals

- 10 repetitions of first 2 counts, unsecured hold

- 10 repetitions of first 4 counts, unsecured hold
- 10 repetitions of 6 counts, unsecured hold
- 10 repetitions of entire sequence in response to defender's cue, unsecured hold
- 10 repetitions of first 2 counts, secured hold
- 10 repetitions of first 4 counts, secured hold
- 10 repetitions of 6 counts, secured hold
- 10 repetitions of entire sequence in response to defender's cue, secured hold

To Decrease Difficulty

- Slow down both grabs and responses. Build the technique more gradually, allowing for a greater number of repetitions at each stage before progressing to the next.

To Increase Difficulty

- Have students try to respond as soon as they sense that they are about to be grabbed, so that the roll-down is executed before the attacker actually plants his or her forearm.
- Encourage more rapid (while still accurate and controlled) follow-up jabs and kicks.

2. *Adding Stressors Drill*

[Corresponds to *Self-Defense*, Step 11, Drill 2]

Group Management and Safety Tips

- Same as for Drill 1

Instructions and Cues to Class

- "To give defenders further opportunity to develop skill in implementing the appropriate defensive tactics despite alarm and momentary disorientation, attackers should shout loudly as they grab, 'Shut up!' or 'Don't move!' The attacker can use either version of the mugger's hold during the 10 repetitions of this exercise."
- "Now do 10 repetitions with the attacker deciding when to attack."

- "Finally, defenders, begin with eyes closed, so that you have no warning of the attack before you are actually grabbed. Once grabbed, open your eyes immediately and then execute the defense. Do this 10 times."

Student Options

- N/A

Student Success Goals

- 10 repetitions with attacker shouting with each grab
- 10 repetitions with attacker determining when to attack
- 10 repetitions of attacks initiated with defender's eyes closed

To Decrease Difficulty

- Slow down both grabs and responses.
- Allow for more repetitions at each stage before moving on to the next.

To Increase Difficulty

- Have students try to respond as soon as they sense they are about to be grabbed.
- Encourage more rapid (while still accurate and controlled) follow-up jabs and kicks.

3. *Moving Attack Drill*
[Corresponds to *Self-Defense*, Step 11, Drill 3]

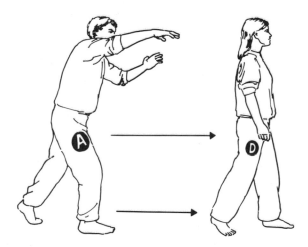

Group Management and Safety Tips

- Same as for Drill 1

Instructions and Cues to Class

- "Defenders, move slowly across the floor and away from attackers. Attackers, when I drop my arm, run up behind a defender and do a controlled grab. Strike with sufficient momentum to slightly accelerate the defender's forward movement but not so much that the defender is knocked to the ground or injured." (*Note:* Those with chronic back or neck injuries should sit out this drill.)
- "Defenders, go with the force until you are able to assume a solid, braced stance. When you have stabilized, execute the response."
- "Repeat until you have attacked and defended 10 times."

Student Option

- "With each repetition of this exercise, defenders should indicate whether, in subsequent grabs, force at impact should be reduced, maintained, or increased."

Student Success Goal

- 8 out of 10 successful applications in response to moving attacks

To Decrease Difficulty

- Slow down both grabs and responses.
- Allow for more repetitions at each stage before moving to the next.

To Increase Difficulty

- Have students try to respond as soon as they sense they are about to be grabbed.
- Encourage more rapid (while still accurate and controlled) follow-up jabs and kicks.

Step 12 Response to Rear Bear Hug

In this step, your students will be learning a response to a rear bear hug—a grab attack in which the attacker encircles the defender's trunk, pinning and immobilizing both arms in the process. With two of four body weapons immobilized, the defender is forced to rely on effective and precise use of the lower limbs and the head. The techniques thrown with these remaining body weapons are the four rear-directed counterattacks introduced in Step 7—the back kick, scrape, heel stomp, and head butt.

The back kick, scrape, and heel stomp are generally thrown in one flowing combination, as soon as the defender is able to regain balance after having been grabbed. These painful counterattacks to the leg generally bring the attacker's head forward. At this point, the defender follows up with a head butt, striking with the back of the skull to the now accessible targets on the attacker's face, the nose and chin.

When your students have mastered this particular combination, they will practice the component parts in reverse order. This enables them to focus on transitional elements such as flow, balance, and recovery from one technique while setting up for another. This, in turn, prepares them for a series of improvisational exercises in which they will create two- and three-technique combinations of their own, drawing from all five rear-directed counterattacks. In the final drill for this step, students have an opportunity to respond in unrehearsed fashion to unfamiliar rear approaches using combinations of their own.

As students move from planned and practiced responses to more spontaneous defenses, encourage good control, sharp concentration, and cooperation between partners. All improvisational drills should be done slowly at first, with students increasing speed only when they are able to demonstrate good balance and the consistent use of very light and controlled (i.e., "whisper") touch.

STUDENT KEYS TO SUCCESS

- Regain balance and throw an effective back kick, scrape, and stomp combination, followed by a head butt to the attacker's face.
- Reverse the order of this defense, and effectively execute a head butt, followed by a kick-scrape-stomp combination.
- Create two-technique combinations drawn from the four techniques of response to a rear bear hug.
- Create three-technique combinations drawn from five rear-directed counterattacks to be used in response to unfamiliar rear grab attacks.
- Use all six body weapons (two upper limbs, two lower limbs, head, and voice) in response to any attack from behind.

Response to Rear Bear Hug Rating

BEGINNING LEVEL	SKILLED LEVEL
• Responds to grab by bending at the waist or losing balance • Rushes the set-up of lower limb technique resulting in loss of balance, power, or accuracy • Has difficulty adapting the defense to changes in circumstances (e.g., height of attacker) • Can execute patterns and combinations as directed by instructor, but has difficulty improvising or figuring out appropriate responses to unfamiliar grab attacks	• Recovers balance quickly and maintains erect posture • Takes time to set up technique and sight target before delivering the counterattack • Modifies and adapts the defense as needed in order to respond effectively to rear bear hug attacks from all manner and sizes of assailants • Creates effective combinations of rear-directed counterattacks in response to both familiar and unfamiliar rear grab attacks

Error Detection and Correction in Response to Rear Bear Hug

Given the difficulty in seeing an attacker's body when one is grabbed from behind, inaccurate and imprecise targeting of techniques is the most common error. Poor targeting is exacerbated by insufficient time taken to set up a technique or by loss of balance resulting from poor posture.

ERROR

CORRECTION

1. The student responds to the grab by bending forward at the waist.	1. The student should take a step or more forward as they are grabbed to better absorb and displace the force of being struck from behind. The spine should stay erect.
2. The student consistently misses targets.	2. The student should take a second longer to properly set up each technique and to sight the targets, actually turning the head and looking in the direction of the targets (even if the target itself is obscured by the assailant's or the student's body). A student who is losing balance during delivery of lower limb technique must "anchor" the upper body during execution. For example, to set up the back kick, the student pikes slightly forward at the hips while keeping spine straight and then prohibits further movement of the upper body away from the target during delivery.

Response to Bear Hug Drills

1. Slow Speed Drill With Partner

[Corresponds to *Self-Defense*, Step 12, Drill 1]

Group Management and Safety Tips

- Have students select partners, then form two parallel lines, both facing out in the same direction. The students in front are designated the defenders and assume a defensive stance. Students in the back row should stand directly behind their partners.
- Make sure students have sufficient room to perform without risk of kicking or being kicked on either side.
- Instruct each student playing attacker to encircle the defender's trunk in a bear hug and pin the defender's arms along the body. The defender's arms should be secured at or below elbow level.
- Remind defenders to use extra caution in using this technique, given the extremely close range at which they are working. The level of contact to be used is very light, a "whisper touch". This allows the defender to practice precise targeting while preventing injury to the attacker.
- Emphasize the importance of looking toward the target to aid in controlling the trajectory and degree of impact, as well as in insuring an accurate strike.
- Because even light contact to the nose can be painful, attackers should move their heads to one side as their partners deliver head butts.

Equipment

- Large mat (for Student Options)
- Tape (for Student Options)

Instructions and Cues to Class

- "You'll be practicing this response to a bear hug at very slow speed and with barely perceptible contact, called 'whisper touch.' This is so you can get an accurate feel for aiming at and impacting on precise targets, but not hurt your partner in the process."

- "The combination you'll be practicing begins with a back kick to the attacker's knee, continues with a scrape down the attacker's shin with either your heel or the blade edge of your foot, and is followed by a heel stomp to the attacker's instep. Theoretically, this should cause the attacker's head to move forward (toward the site of the pain). When you feel this happening, throw your head back to butt the attacker's nose or chin. Repeat this combination 15 times, taking care to move slowly and touch softly."

Student Options

- "Do an impact drill using the kick-scrape-stomp series. Place a large mat on end against a wall; you may need to have someone hold it in place. Then tape a large X at knee level, add a vertical strip just below it to designate a shin, and tape an X on the floor directly below and in front of the strip to designate an instep. Start with very light impact, and build up to no more than half speed to avoid bruising your heel. This drill is useful in developing accurate aim and in learning how to maintain balance even as you are striking a target."

Student Success Goal

- 15 slow speed repetitions of the entire sequence, as initially presented

To Decrease Difficulty

- First have students try the combination without a partner. Encourage them to take their time and move slowly through the sequence, throwing each technique to an imaginary target.
- If students are having trouble keeping their balance, have them rest their hands on the back of a chair or a wall directly in front of

them (see Figure 12.1). This way, they can concentrate on set-ups, trajectories, and targets without worrying about maintaining balance. After a number of repetitions, have them grab the chair only when they lose balance. Later, remove the chair.

Figure 12.1 To Decrease Difficulty: Have students rest their hands on the back of a chair or against a wall so they can concentrate on set-ups, trajectories, and targets.

To Increase Difficulty

- If students are able to execute defense well from a stationary stance, have them try a "mobile defense." Instruct defenders to walk away from attackers. On your signal, attackers run up behind defenders and grab them in a bear hug. Remind defenders to take as many steps forward as necessary when they are hit to regain balance and assume a stable stance. "Joining" with the force generated by an attacker running up behind and grabbing prevents the defender from being knocked to the ground. As soon as the defender is able to assume a solid stance, she or he executes the defense. *Caution:* Defensive sequences should be done at half speed and should stop short of actual impact on a partner's body.

2. *Reverse Order and Flexible Response Drill*
[Corresponds to *Self-Defense*, Step 12, Drill 2]

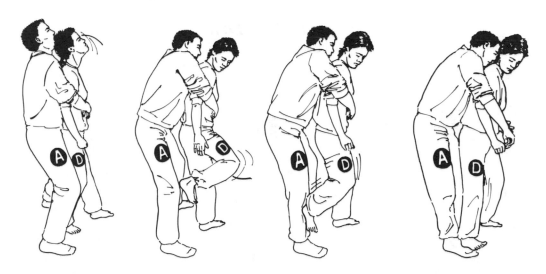

Group Management and Safety Tips

- Use the Group Management and Safety Tips for Drill 1.

Instructions and Cues to Class

- "This drill is the first in a number to help you develop greater flexibility in the use of rear-directed counterattacks. In this exercise, change the response so that the head butt precedes the kick-scrape-stomp. Practice this reverse order, slow-speed response to the bear hug 15 times, or until you are able to deliver it in a balanced, effective manner."

• "Now try experimenting with different two-technique combinations, drawing from the four techniques used to counter a rear bear hug. For example, you could do a head butt-heel stomp combination or a scrape-stomp combination. Try several combinations and note those that work well (Does the second technique flow easily and fluidly from the first?). See if you can come up with six combinations, and then do 5 repetitions of each."

Student Options

• N/A

Student Success Goals

• 15 repetitions of head butt followed by kick-scrape-stomp
• 5 repetitions each of at least six different two-technique combinations

To Decrease Difficulty

• Encourage students to work at slow speed and without a partner while practicing the reverse order and two-technique combinations. Sometimes watching another pair of students for a few minutes can help a student who is having difficulty coming up with appropriate combinations. Or you can provide a few examples (e.g., heel stomp-head butt) to get them started.

To Increase Difficulty

• Try using the "milling" format used in earlier steps. Students mill rapidly around the room, taking care to keep approximately 2 arms'-lengths between themselves and all others. At any point, any student can grab another in a rear bear hug. The grabbed student responds with the defense as first presented or in reverse order, or with an improvised two-technique combination. Attackers should say something menacing when they grab (e.g., "Come with me," or "Don't say a word "). Defenders should ki-yai on each technique.

Again, remind students to respond at half speed only and to stop short of actual impact on a partner's body. Also remind them to exercise special care when executing head butts.

3. Grab-Bag Drill
[Corresponds to *Self-Defense*, Step 12, Drill 3]

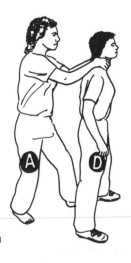
a

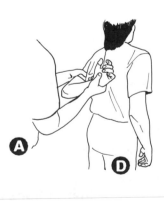
b

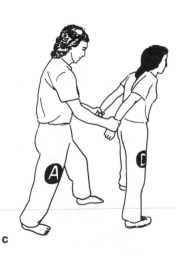
c

Group Management and Safety Tips

- Introduce the first of the unfamiliar rear grab attacks, the rear choke hold (a). Then ask students to identify (1) accessible targets on the attacker's body, (2) body weapons available to the defender, and (3) rear-directed counterattacks that are good prospects for defense. Repeat this process as you introduce the next two unfamiliar grabs, the arm bar (b) and the double wrist grab (c). Use the Rear Grab Defense Chart as a reference for your discussion.
- Have students select partners, and have defenders and attackers form parallel lines, as in previous drills in this step.
- Make sure that each pair has sufficient room to perform without interfering with those around them.
- Make sure there is only "whisper touch" level of contact.
- Emphasize the importance of defenders' looking in the direction of the target.
- Instruct attackers to move their heads to one side or another as their partners deliver head butts.
- Monitor students' speed and control throughout this improvisational exercise. When everyone has developed a response, allow some or all to present their combinations to the group.

Instructions and Cues to Class

- "In this drill, you will be creating your own responses to three rear grab attacks not previously discussed in this class. Drawing on skills you've already learned, you'll decide which combinations of the rear-directed counterattacks might be effective in response to a rear choke, an arm bar, and, finally, a double wrist grab from behind."
- "Throughout this drill move at slow speed, use whisper touch, and generally exercise caution as you experiment with different defenses. To determine which technique might reasonably follow the one you have just done, have your partner move his or her head *toward* the point of impact. Note which targets open up and which body weapons you have still available. This should help you decide your next move."
- (After introduction of rear choke hold and discussion of targets, weapons, and pos-

sible techniques) "Now experiment with a few different two- and three-technique combinations until you find one that *flows* as a response to this grab attack. Then repeat that combination a minimum of five times."
- "We'll be repeating this process with arm bars and double wrist grabs from behind."

Student Option

- "Try to think of other rear grab attacks. Develop combinations of rear-directed counterattacks that could be used to defend against them."

Student Success Goals

- 5 repetitions of a two- or three-technique combination in response to a rear choke hold
- 5 repetitions of a two- or three-technique combination in response to an arm bar
- 5 repetitions of a two- or three-technique combination in response to a double wrist grab from behind

To Decrease Difficulty

- Sometimes students who have difficulty seeing possibilities for defense when they are playing defender will see those possibilities more readily as an observer. Have these students watch as someone else is grabbed. Then have them suggest techniques for the defender to try, given any accessible targets on the attacker's body and the body weapons available to defender. When they are comfortable creating combinations in this manner, have them resume the role of defender and implement these combinations themselves.

To Increase Difficulty

- Adapt this drill to a milling format. Students mill around the workout space, taking care to maintain their critical distance zones. Any student can grab another, using *any* rear grab attack. Defenders respond to each attack with a two- or three-technique combination of their choice, incorporating any of the five rear-directed counterattacks.

  Note: Remind your students to exercise caution, move slowly, and either touch lightly or stop short of actual contact to an attacker's body.

Rear Grab Defense Chart

Rear grab	Accessible targets	Available body weapons	Possible techniques
Rear bear hug	Face	Head	Head butt
	Knee	Lower limbs	Back kick
	Shin	Lower limbs	Scrape
	Instep	Lower limbs	Stomp
Rear choke hold	Solar plexus	Upper limbs	Elbow jab
	Ribs	Upper limbs	Elbow jab
	Knee	Lower limbs	Back kick
	Shin	Lower limbs	Scrape
	Instep	Lower limbs	Stomp
Arm bar*	Face	Head	Head butt
	Knee	Lower limbs	Back kick
	Shin	Lower limbs	Scrape
	Instep	Lower limbs	Stomp
Double wrist grab	Face	Head	Head butt
	Knee	Lower limbs	Back kick
	Shin	Lower limbs	Scrape
	Instep	Lower limbs	Stomp

*Note: It may be possible for a defender to use his or her free arm to throw an elbow jab (or a groin strike, for that matter) if the arm bar is not too severe. However, if the restrained arm is so firmly pinned that the defender's back is arched, effective execution of an elbow jab is unlikely.

Step 13   Response to Wrist Grabs

Your students are now ready to practice *quick releases* in response to being grabbed by one or both wrists. Although wrist grabs don't elicit the fear that choke holds and full-body grabs do, they are nonetheless dangerous in that a defender can be pulled into a more restrictive or risky situation by the attacker (e.g., into a car, a deserted room or office, or toward a less trafficked area).

You'll be teaching your students responses to three wrist grab variations: a one-handed grab by an attacker to one of the defender's wrists; a two-handed grab by the attacker of both of the defender's wrists; and a two-handed grab by the attacker of one of the defender's wrists. Refer to these grabs as 1-on-1, 2-on-2, and 2-on-1, respectively.

As you introduce these grabs to your students, emphasize that the more powerful the assailant's grip, the more important it is that the defender understand and correctly apply a few basic principles governing the breaking of these holds. Point out that in all three defenses

- force must be concentrated against the assailant's thumb(s), rather than fingers,
- the force used to break the hold is generated by powerful rotation of the defender's trunk,
- the defender can generate even greater force by using both arms to break the hold, even when only one wrist is grabbed, and
- with correct application of these principles, a relatively small defender can often break the grip of a larger, stronger attacker.

When students have mastered the quick releases for all three grab variations, you'll be introducing preliminary moves—distraction techniques that increase the likelihood of successful release when the attacker's grip is very powerful. The distraction techniques practiced in Drill 2, the Split-Focus Drill, are three of the front-facing strikes—front snap kicks, palm-heel strikes, and web strikes.

In Drill 3, the Strike Follow-Up Drill, you'll be teaching responses to assault situations in which the defender needs to follow up a quick release with a counterattack in order to discourage an attacker from pressing an assault. Specific follow-up techniques that students will practice include punches, hammerfists, and side stomp kicks.

Finally, in Drill 4, students will learn to sandwich a wrist release between a distraction technique and a follow-up strike.

In the last three drills, students will advance from designated responses to improvised responses. The designated responses are designed for flow and efficiency of movement, particularly through the transitions. Instruct students to pay particular attention to these elements as they create their own combinations of moves. And, as with all improvisational drills, encourage caution, control, and cooperation as students explore the process of creating their own defenses.

STUDENT KEYS TO SUCCESS

- Correctly execute quick releases in response to three variations of wrist grabs: 1-on-1, 2-on-2, and 2-on-1 grabs.
- Incorporate front-facing strikes to split the attacker's focus and loosen his or her grip just before an attempted break.
- Follow up the break with appropriate and accurately targeted counterattacks to discourage the attacker from pressing the assault.
- Move easily and fluidly from distraction technique through wrist release to follow-up technique.
- Create effective responses to wrist grabs by incorporating distractions, releases, and appropriate follow-ups.

Response to Wrist Grabs Rating

BEGINNING LEVEL	SKILLED LEVEL
• Attempts to slowly pry or wrestle wrist free from attacker; strains against attacker's grip • Occasionally allows wrists to bend while attempting the break • Uses incorrect posture and alignment, occasionally bending forward at the waist and using trunk extension to break holds • Frequently attempts to break against attacker's fingers rather than thumb • Moves slowly and somewhat awkwardly from distraction through break and follow-up • Occasionally misses targets or throws counterattacks to inappropriate targets when using distractions or follow-ups	• Uses explosive, ballistic movement to break hold • Consistently maintains a straight wrist line while breaking hold • Maintains erect, upright posture and incorporates trunk rotation to break holds • Consistently opposes attacker's thumb • Moves smoothly and quickly through transitions between moves • Impacts targets precisely; uses appropriate counterattacks for each target

Error Detection and Correction in Wrist Releases

Common errors are those that violate the principles outlined earlier. Carefully monitor students to make sure that they are not forgetting trunk rotation and using only their arms to power the break, opposing the attacker's fingers rather than thumb, or using only one arm to break the hold when two are necessary. Other errors are often related to improper grip (e.g., a bent wrist or laced fingers).

ERROR

CORRECTION

ERROR	CORRECTION
1. The student's wrists are bent.	1. Point out that a bent wrist weakens the effort to break the hold and greatly increases the risk of a wrist sprain. If necessary, splint the wrist with a ruler or tongue depressor and have the student do a few releases this way to feel the difference in ease and effectiveness of the break.

ERROR   **CORRECTION**

2. The student straightens his or her arms on the set-up and brings them straight overhead on the break.

2. It's possible to injure the shoulders when doing the break this way. Have the student bend his or her elbows at 90 degrees on the set-up, then yank fists explosively to the butt of the shoulder to break the attacker's hold. Point out that at the completion of the break, elbows should be fully flexed with fists in front of the shoulder.

3. The student is bending at the waist just before the break.

3. The student is relying on lower back muscles to break the hold, which could easily result in a serious muscle pull. Instead, the student should focus on rotating the trunk while maintaining erect posture and vertical alignment.

4. After breaking 2-on-2 and 2-on-1 grabs, the student brings his or her freed hands to the lead shoulder.

4. This move restricts the degree of trunk rotation, thus weakening the break attempt, and twists the spine uncomfortably. Have the student practice bringing freed hands to the rear (i.e., trailing) shoulder.

5. The student laces the fingers together instead of covering one fist with the other.

5. Remind the student that fingers can be crushed and injured when laced in this fashion. Have student practice the correct position—one fist gripping the other—until it becomes automatic.

Wrist Release Drills

1. *Quick-Release Drill*
[Corresponds to *Self-Defense*, Step 13, Drill 1]

Group Management and Safety Tips

- Have students select partners and form two parallel lines, partners facing one another in defensive stances.
- Make certain that students have sufficient room to perform this drill without risk of striking their neighbors with a flailing arm.

- Instruct the attacking students to do 15 repetitions each of 1-on-1, then 2-on-2, then 2-on-1 wrist grabs. Remind them that the 1-on-1 grabs can be either mirror-image or cross-body grabs. Finally, instruct attackers to do 15 additional grabs, randomly mixing the three variations.

- Because of the high number of repetitions involving smaller body parts (i.e., wrists), wrist sprains, skin burns, and abrasions are possible. To reduce this likelihood, have attackers use very light grips only.

Instructions and Cues to Class

- "This drill is designed to help you increase the quickness of your response to three variations of a wrist grab. Each time you are grabbed, note the position of the attacker's thumb, identify the appropriate release, and execute the break. On each successive grab, try to respond more quickly than the time before. Repeat until your releases are explosive and immediate."
- "Do this in response to 1-on-1, 2-on-2, and finally 2-on-1 grabs. Then challenge yourself even further with a random-order drill in which your partner uses all three grabs."
- "When finished, switch roles and repeat the drill."

Student Options

- N/A

Student Success Goals

- 13 out of 15 correctly executed wrist releases in response to 1-on-1 grabs
- 13 out of 15 correctly executed wrist releases in response to 2-on-2 grabs
- 13 out of 15 correctly executed wrist releases in response to 2-on-1 grabs
- 13 out of 15 correctly executed wrist releases in response to the 3 grab variations done in random order

To Decrease Difficulty

- Have attacker use an even lighter grip. Allow defenders to take all the time they need to determine location of the thumb and the appropriate break trajectory. Increase speed more gradually and over a larger number of repetitions.

To Increase Difficulty

- Allow less time for defender to react.

2. *Split-Focus Drill*
[Corresponds to *Self-Defense*, Step 13, Drill 2]

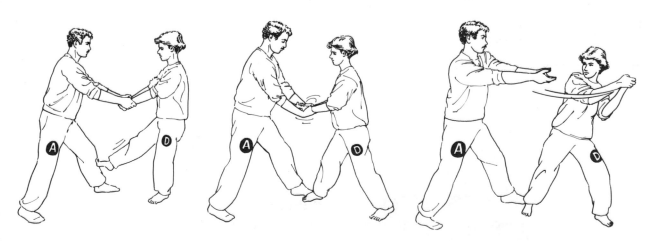

Group Management and Safety Tips

- As before, have students form two parallel lines, with partners facing one another in defensive stances. Be sure that there is sufficient space available for students to execute moves without inadvertently striking pairs practicing nearby.

- Instruct attackers to use a light grip, given the high number of repetitions to be done.
- Continually remind defenders to exercise caution and control in executing strikes and kicks: All strikes should be pulled a few inches short of actual targets, and kicks should be thrown off to the side of actual knees and shins.

Instructions and Cues to Class

- "In this drill, you'll incorporate distraction techniques into your responses to wrist grabs. Distractions are useful in situations where the strength of the attacker's grip precludes a simple break. The purpose of the distraction is to draw an attacker's attention elsewhere, thereby causing him or her to loosen the grip. At the instant that the grip is loosened, the defender executes the release."
- "There are a range of techniques available for use as distractions, ranging from complete relaxation of the wrist being held to potentially deadly counterattacks, such as the web strike to the throat. Selection of a distraction technique is based on what is necessary (What is the degree of threat?) and possible (Which targets are accessible? Which body weapons are available?)."
- "Know that there are also psychological distractions, such as a sharp glance behind the attacker as if to suggest that someone is there. Or, something in the environment may momentarily startle and cause an attacker to lose focus (e.g., a dog barking, a telephone ringing, a car backfiring, etc.)."
- "In response to a 2-on-2 grab, which ties up both of your hands, throw a front snap kick to the attacker's shin. When the attacker responds to the kick, namely by loosening his or her grip, instantly execute the appropriate release. Repeat this combination of distraction-release 10 times or until you are able to move smoothly and quickly from the kick into the release."

- "Practice each of the combinations I will suggest. Then try creating a few combinations of distraction-release on your own. Practice each combination until you can do it in a balanced, fluid manner. As you do these, keep in mind that in an actual assault, you would select a distraction technique that was both *possible* (based on targets and body weapons available) and *necessary* in a given situation."

Student Options

- N/A

Student Success Goals

- 10 front snap kicks to shin followed by wrist release (2-on-2 grab)
- 10 front snap kicks to knee followed by wrist release (2-on-2 grab)
- 10 palm-heel strikes to nose followed by wrist release (1-on-1 grab)
- 10 web strikes to throat followed by wrist release (1-on-1 grab)
- 10 distraction of student's choosing followed by wrist release

To Decrease Difficulty

- Slow drills down. Give students plenty of time to figure out appropriate techniques. To facilitate this, keep reminding students to look for accessible targets and available body weapons. Do extra repetitions of each drill until moves are correctly and fluidly executed.

To Increase Difficulty

- Have defenders try to increase their speed of response.

3. Strike Follow-Up Drill
[Corresponds to *Self-Defense*, Step 13, Drill 3]

Group Management and Safety Tips

- Align the group as in Drill 1: partners in parallel lines and facing one another.
- Make sure there is enough room for each pair to perform the drill without striking other students practicing nearby.

Instructions and Cues to Class

- "Now that you are competent in using distraction techniques *before* you attempt the release, add a counterattack *after* you have broken the attacker's grip. The purpose of this follow-up strike is to discourage the

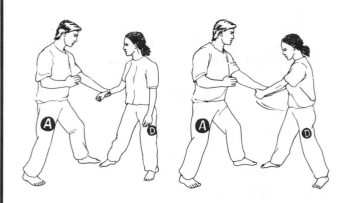
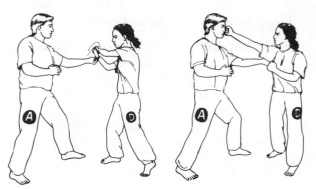

attacker from pressing the assault. Follow-ups are usually front-facing or side-directed counterattacks, selected for the ease they can be used with a particular release. Do 10 of each of the following release–follow-up combinations, and then create 10 of your own:

   a. Release of a 1-on-1 grab followed by a punch to the nose with the trailing hand (illustrated above)

   b. Release of a 2-on-2 grab followed by a hammerfist to the attacker's nose, temple, jaw, or neck (This side-directed strike is possible because the powerful trunk rotation used to power the release leaves one side toward the attacker; this is the side from which the hammerfist is thrown.)

   c. Release of a 2-on-1 grab followed by a side stomp kick to the knee (Note that a side-directed counterattack is possible, because completing the break leaves the defender in a side stance, the preparatory position for a side stomp kick to the nearest knee.)"

- "Work for balance, fluidity, and control as you practice these release–follow-up combinations and those that you create."

Student Option

- "Create your own combinations."

Student Success Goals

- 10 1-on-1 releases plus follow-up punches to nose
- 10 2-on-2 releases plus follow-up hammerfists
- 10 2-on-1 releases plus follow-up side stomp kicks
- 10 appropriate releases plus follow-ups of student's choice

To Decrease Difficulty

- Slow drills down. Allow more time for determining accessible targets and available body weapons for use in follow-up.

To Increase Difficulty

- Have students add a second follow-up technique. Encourage them to develop combinations that are fluid (flow easily from one to the next) and efficient (require minimal changes in stance and set-up between techniques).

4. *Sandwich Drill*
[Corresponds to *Self-Defense*, Step 13, Drill 4]

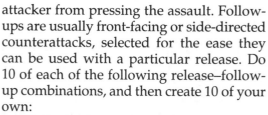

Group Management and Safety Tips

- Align the group as in Drill 1, where partners in parallel lines face one another.
- Make sure there is enough room for each pair to perform the drill without striking those practicing nearby.

Instructions and Cues to Class

- "In this variation, you will 'sandwich' a wrist release between a distraction technique and a follow-up."

- "Like previous drills, first practice these combinations, and then create a few of your own sandwiches:
  a. In response to a 1-on-1 grab
     Distraction: lead-leg front kick to shin
     Release: 1-on-1 release
     Follow-up: trailing-hand palm-heel strike
  b. In response to the 2-on-2 grab
     Distraction: lead-leg front kick to shin
     Release: 2-on-2 release
     Follow-up: hammerfist
  c. In response to a 2-on-1 grab
     Distraction: trailing-hand palm-heel strike
     Release: 2-on-1 release
     Follow-up: side stomp kick to nearest knee"
     (illustrated above)
- "Don't rush through these three-part combinations. Work for accurate, well-executed strikes; effective, explosive releases; and fluid transitions as you move from the preliminary move through the break to the follow-up."

Student Option

- "Create your own sandwiches."

Student Success Goals

- 10 repetitions of designated response to 1-on-1 grab
- 10 repetitions of designated response to 2-on-2 grab
- 10 repetitions of designated response to 2-on-1 grab
- 10 responses (incorporating both a distraction and a follow-up of student's choosing) to random wrist grabs

To Decrease Difficulty

- Slow execution down, particularly if students are rushing through the three components of the sandwich. Have them look at where each component leaves them and discuss how to move from that position into the next component, smoothly and efficiently.
- Have students watch others in order to gather ideas before trying to improvise defenses of their own.
- Divide students into teams of three and have them work together to create a few "sandwiches." This reduces the stress that improvisational drills invoke in some students.

To Increase Difficulty

- Have students mill around randomly, taking care to keep a distance of 2 arms'-lengths from everyone. Anyone can play attacker by suddenly pointing at another and shouting, "You!" Both students freeze for an instant, then the attacker grabs the defender with any one of the three grab variations. For the first minute, have the defender just execute the appropriate release; during the second minute of milling, add a distraction technique; during the third minute, a follow-up. To insure everyone's safety, emphasize caution, a light grip on grabs, and stopping short of targets on all counterattacks. Afterwards, have people demonstrate their most effective or unusual innovations.

Step 14   Recall Under Stress

The ability to stay calm and to maintain presence of mind in a threatening or assaultive situation is a critical self-defense skill. Without this, even the most physically adept student will be hard pressed to make sound, swift decisions about defense options when an emergency of this sort occurs. The drills presented in this step are designed to increase your students' ability to accurately and quickly assess specific situational and positional factors, rapidly weigh options and risks, and select and then implement appropriate and well-timed defenses—all while keeping panic and fear at bay.

The increasing levels of spontaneity and unpredictability in these drills place ever greater demands on students' observation, judgment, and performance skills. They will be responding to random attacks, thrown by a succession of attackers (of different limb lengths, sizes, shapes, energy, speed, intensity) and from different angles and ranges. And they will be doing all of this, finally, in a role play based on circumstances that they identify as being particularly unnerving and frightening to them.

Participating in the drills in this step will increase students' capacities for calm, clear, and strategic thinking in responding to the emergency of assault. In the process, students will also have an opportunity to review and practice the entire range of defenses presented in this class.

STUDENT KEYS TO SUCCESS

- Accurately and quickly assess specific situational and positional factors.
- Identify options, and select and implement appropriate and effective defenses.
- Maintain a calm, focused state of mind.
- Demonstrate competence in entire range of skills (e.g., assertiveness/confrontation, de-escalation, all physical techniques) presented in this book.
- Adapt defenses, as needed, in order to respond effectively to attackers of different sizes and shapes and to attacks of different speeds and intensities.

Recall Under Stress Rating

Anyone, on being suddenly grabbed or struck, is momentarily shocked and startled. In the seconds immediately following a physical attack, some people get stuck in panic, confusion, terror, rage, physical pain, nausea, dissociation, and denial. Others recover quickly from the startled response and slip instantly into problem solving—figuring out what they need to do in order

to deter the assailant. With training and practice, this becomes the more likely response.

The Recall Under Stress Rating Chart lists possible reactions in an untrained and a trained individual to sudden attack. Note that both will initially experience shock and momentary disorientation. What follows that startled response is what is important.

Recall Under Stress Rating

BEGINNING LEVEL	ADVANCED LEVEL
• Flails wildly, or freezes	• Overcomes initial panic quickly and focuses on details of defense (i.e., assesses situation, chooses and implements appropriate response)
• Throws poorly executed technique; misses targets	• Correctly executes technique; strikes designated targets
• Blanks on possible responses, or is unable to recall possible defenses	• Stays focused and responsive to constantly shifting scene

Recall Under Stress Drills

1. 5-for-5 Drill

[Corresponds to *Self-Defense*, Step 14, Drill 1]

Group Management and Safety Tips

- Have students select partners and face one another in defensive stances.
- Make certain that there is approximately 10 feet between each pair of students to allow sufficient room for circling, maneuvering, and trading attacks without inadvertently striking others practicing nearby.
- Instruct attackers and defenders to maintain an awareness of other people practicing nearby in order to avoid collisions while circling.
- Have pairs gradually increase speed during this drill, while taking care not to go so fast that they are unable to control their strikes or to exercise restraint on the push-away used with the flying wedge.

Instructions and Cues to Class

- "The purpose of this drill is to learn how to adapt to changing angles of attack and to the uncertainty of knowing just when the attack will be launched. The drill progresses from predetermined attacks to attacks in which the defender will not know what kind of attack is coming until it has been launched."

- "To start, the attacker will launch the first designated attack, a lunging punch, five times. The defender will respond each time with an evasive sidestep. Attackers, be sure to take a few seconds to circle and maneuver for position between attacks. During this time, defenders should remain alert and centered and prepare for the next attack. After five exchanges, reverse roles, with the new attacker throwing the same attack five times. When both partners have responded to this first designated attack (a lunging punch) with the designated defense (an evasive sidestep), trade 5-for-5 of these attacks and defenses:

Attack	Defense
Attempted front choke hold	Flying wedge + push-away
Secured front choke hold	Kick-flying wedge-palm-heel strike
Wrist grabs (any variation)	Quick wrist releases"

- "When you've practiced all four designated attacks and defenses in this manner, do at least one more set of five attacks. In this exchange, the attacker chooses the attacks, drawn at random from those already practiced. The defender must now quickly determine the nature of the attack and respond accordingly. Continue trading 5-for-5 until both of you are consistently and effectively responding 5 out of 5 times."

Student Option

- "A challenging variation on this drill is to go from trading 5-for-5 to 4-for-4 to 3-for-3 to 2-for-2 until you are trading 1-for-1. Do this over a period of 5 minutes, so that you spend 1 full minute at each step. While you are trading 1-for-1, you'll be moving rapidly from offense to defense and back again, which requires intense concentration and control, and more accurately resembles actual fight dynamics."

Student Success Goals

- 5 successful responses to lunging punches
- 5 successful responses to attempted front choke holds
- 5 successful responses to secured front choke holds
- 5 successful responses to wrist grabs
- 5 successful responses to random attacks

To Decrease Difficulty

- Slow attacks down
- Have attacker alert the defender as to the nature of the impending attack by giving more obvious and elaborate cues. This can be done by
  a. placing a fisted hand in front of the shoulder to suggest that a lunge punch is coming;
  b. placing open hands in front of the chest in preparation for an attempted front choke hold;
  c. keeping hands low and at the side of the body to indicate that a wrist grab is likely (see Figure 14.1).

Direct the defenders' attention to the ways in which attackers telegraph their moves. With practice, defenders should become more skilled at reading significant cues to the nature of the impending attack. As defenders become more proficient at this, attackers can be less obvious about how they intend to attack.

Figure 14.1   To Decrease Difficulty: Have attackers telegraph their moves.

To Increase Difficulty

- Increase speed of attacks.
- Reduce length of pause between attacks.
- Minimize telegraphing on the part of attacker (i.e., have attacker try to minimize any preliminary moves that suggest a particular attack to the defender).

2. Challenge Line

[Corresponds to *Self-Defense*, Step 14, Drill 2]

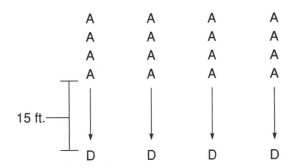

Group Management and Safety Tips

- Have students form teams of five people, and line up, one behind the other. Then have one team member stand about 15 feet out in front of the others, facing them.
- Explain that this drill will provide an opportunity to practice the same defense against a number of people (i.e., the other four members of the team). Like the previous drill, attacks will first be predetermined, and eventually, random.
- Emphasize that only one team member attacks at a time and that before an attacker breaks from the line, she or he *must* make eye contact with the defender.
- Attackers will move quickly toward defenders but should be careful not to overwhelm or run right over them. (This should be a controlled charge.)
- Point out that when the designated attack is a rear grab, defenders should stand with their backs to the attacking team. Again, the attack should be controlled and not knock the defenders off-balance.
- When team members have practiced all the designated attacks and defenses, repeat the drill using random attacks. To avoid confusion, have attackers select from the three *front*-facing attacks used previously in the drill.
- Early during the random-attack portion of the drill, have attackers telegraph their intentions by using obvious and somewhat elaborate set-ups for particular attacks, like they did in Drill 1. (See "To Decrease Difficulty" in Drill 1.)

Instructions and Cues to Class

- "One at a time, each member of your team will break from the line and launch the same predetermined attack. When the person standing out front has defended against this attack from all four team members, she or he moves to the back of the line. The team member previously at the head of the line now becomes the defender, assumes the position out front, and prepares to defend against the same attack. Repeat this process until all team members have had a chance to play defender."
- "When the first defender is again out front, repeat the drill using the next designated attack and defense. Repeat the drill until your team has moved through all of these attack-defense combinations:

Attack	Defense
Lunging punch	Evasive sidestep
Attempted front choke hold	Flying wedge-push-away
Wrist grab (any variation)	Quick wrist releases
Mugger's hold	Release-elbow-kick
Rear bear hug	Kick-scrape-stomp-head butt"

- "Finally, remember to exercise caution and control during this challenging and somewhat fast-paced drill."

Student Options

- "A variation on this drill has the four team members forming a gauntlet as illustrated in Figure 14.2."

Figure 14.2   Student Option: The gauntlet.

- "The defender moves from team member to team member, alternating from side to side as diagrammed, and responds to the same attack until he or she reaches the end of the gauntlet. The defender then assumes a position on either side to become one of the attackers, and the person at the head of the gauntlet becomes the next defender. When each person has run the gauntlet and responded to the same attack, repeat the process with the next of the designated attacks and defenses. Finally, repeat the drill using random front-facing attacks."
- "The gauntlet is slightly more stressful and demanding than the Challenge Line, given the closer proximity of the attacker to the defender. Whereas the Challenge Line has the attacker crossing a distance of 15 feet to get to the defender, the gauntlet places each attacker only a few feet from the defender. This requires an even quicker reading of the attacker's intentions and more rapid implementation of the appropriate response by the defender."

Student Success Goals

- 4 effective responses to lunging punches (assumes 4 attackers)
- 4 effective responses to attempted front choke holds
- 4 effective responses to wrist grab variations
- 4 effective responses to mugger's holds
- 4 effective responses to rear bear hugs
- 4 effective responses to random front-facing attacks (e.g., lunging punches, attempted front choke holds, wrist grabs)

To Decrease Difficulty

- Slow the drill down; encourage more elaborate telegraphing on the part of the attacker.

To Increase Difficulty

- Increase speed, minimize telegraphing, and reduce distance between the attacker and the defender.

3. Milling Drill

[Corresponds to *Self-Defense*, Step 14, Drill 3]

Group Management and Safety Tips

- Have students spread out so that there is a minimum distance of 2 arms'-lengths between them.
- Instruct students to mill randomly and rapidly around the room maintaining critical distance from all others.
- Remind students that anyone can be an attacker simply by shouting "You!" while pointing at another student. Immediately, both attacker and defender freeze for a moment before the attacker launches the attack. After the defender responds, both begin to mill once again until either chooses to attack or is called to defend.
- Suggest to students that attacks be slower during the first half minute of the drill. This allows participants to become comfortable with the format before speed and intensity increase.
- Remind students to allow plenty of space for sudden direction changes and increasingly rapid movement and to avoid collisions.
- When you have reviewed general rules for milling, point out that in this 3-minute version, students will defend against ever more types of attacks from a variety of attackers. Though only one familiar attack and defense will be done during the first 30 seconds, another attack and defense will be added each half minute until a defender may be using any one of five defenses.
- Finally, in the last half minute of this drill, defenders will be drawing on their knowledge of self-defense to respond to unfamiliar attacks by using their own innovative defenses.
- Remind students to use good control at all times, particularly when throwing strike counterattacks or implementing unfamiliar and unpracticed attacks or defenses in the last 30 seconds of this drill.

Instructions and Cues to Class

- "For the first 30 seconds of this drill, attackers will use only lunging punches, and defenders will respond with evasive side-steps. In the next 30 seconds, an alternative attack is the front choke hold, to which defenders respond with a flying wedge. In the third 30-second period, attackers may also use mugger's holds, without shouting 'You!' Defenders will respond by rolling the attacker's arm down and following up with elbow jabs or back kicks, taking care to stop short of impact on their partner's body. In the fourth 30-second period, attackers may also use wrist grabs, and defenders, the quick releases. In the fifth 30-second period, no new attacks are allowed, but defenders may add front-facing counterattacks as follow-ups to their quick wrist releases."
- "Now, slow your speed considerably. For last 30 seconds of this drill, attackers may use any unarmed grab attack, including those not covered in this book. Defenders, moving at slow speed and drawing from skills learned in this training, will create their own responses. Exercise caution, control, and imagination."

Student Options

- N/A

Student Success Goal

- Effective defenses in response to approximately 90% of attacks during 3-minute milling period

To Decrease Difficulty

- Move at very slow speed.
- Have attacker pause longer before attacking and use more elaborate telegraphs to allow defender maximum time for setting up defense.

To Increase Difficulty

- Increase speed of the drill.
- Have attackers pause for only a split second between shouting and pointing at someone and then attacking. This challenges the defender to set up a defense more quickly.

4. Confronting Your Fear

[Corresponds to *Self-Defense*, Step 14, Drill 4]

Group Management and Safety Tips

- Explain to students that there are two parts to this drill. The first is an imaging exercise, a sort of guided meditation, in which they will lie or sit quietly on the floor and "see" themselves moving through the entire Continuum of Response to successfully defend against an assault. Point out that this exercise is useful for a number of reasons:

  1. By recalling the three A's it reminds students of the avoidance strategies (Awareness) available to them and reinforces the importance of developing observational (Assessment) and judgment (Action) skills in preparing to deal effectively with assault.
  2. It enables students to review the details of preventive strategies, such as De-Escalation and Confrontation/Assertiveness, in stopping an assault before it reaches the point of physical aggression.
  3. It reinforces students' grasp of options available for responding to assault and allows them to mentally rehearse a detailed and successful physical defense.
  4. To the extent that the fantasy reflects a particular fear, it may enable students to lay to rest feelings of powerlessness and vulnerability in certain circumstances.
  5. This drill provides an alternative to simply dismissing or discounting anxiety and fear when they arise in situations where we feel at risk.
  6. It offers a method for ongoing review and practice of the entire range of skills presented in this book.

- The second part of this drill allows students to act out this sequence with a partner. The designated defender in each pair provides the designated attacker with details on how the interaction proceeds from the assessment through the attack. The defender also tells the attacker the planned defense, first the soft self-defense and then the physical techniques. Suggest that defenders see themselves as directors of a

movie scene and have them attend to such things as underlying feelings of the attacker and defender, time of day, location, etc. When this has been thoroughly discussed and described, the pair role-play the entire scene. Emphasize to students that the outcome is *always* the successful deterrence of the assailant. Encourage the pair to discuss the interaction when it has been completed.

Instructions and Cues to Class

- "Identify a potentially dangerous situation that is of special concern to you—a particular route you regularly walk, an acquaintance in whose company you are frequently uneasy, or a set of circumstances such as dealing with an inebriated and coercive date. Recall from Step 1, 'Awareness,' the precautionary measures you might take to reduce your accessibility and vulnerability to this particular assault. See yourself taking these precautions." (Pause here to allow students time to do this.)
- "Now imagine that despite your precautions, you suddenly find yourself in this circumstance. See yourself conducting a rapid *Assessment* of the situation, noting pertinent details about the environment, the threatening individual, and yourself." (Pause. . . .)
- "See yourself decide that *Immediate Retreat* is called for, and note the manner in which you rapidly remove yourself from the situation." (Pause. . . .)
- "Now see yourself deciding that soft self-defense is appropriate. Ask yourself whether this is a sexual assault, and, if so, what stage has been reached. If this is your reading, see yourself using the nonverbal and verbal principles of *Confrontation/Assertiveness*. If, instead of a sexual assailant, this is simply a highly agitated and potentially explosive individual, see yourself applying the nonverbal and verbal principles of *De-Escalation*. Whatever the nature of the threatened assault, see your use of these preventive skills being effective and successful in reducing the likelihood of physical violence." (Pause. . . .)
- "Finally, imagine that despite all your efforts at preventing violence, the person in

your imaginary scenario moves on you. Be precise and detailed as you imagine this: Is the attacker punching? To what part of your body? Is the attacker grabbing? How? From what distance? How fast? See yourself responding with the appropriate neutralizing technique. Determine whether simple retreat is possible at this point or whether counterattack is necessary. See yourself doing whatever you feel is appropriate and then retreating to safety." (Pause. . . .)

- "Now, choose a partner with whom to role-play the entire scene. Provide the details of the interaction, and then act it out. Stick pretty close to your visualized script, and make certain that the final outcome is effective and successful defense in the circumstances you have described. After you have completed the role play, discuss it with your partner. Note where you felt particularly strong and effective. Also note where you felt less capable, and repeat these portions of the role play until you feel more confident."

Student Option

- "Repeat the imaging exercise by 'revisiting' a situation that you have actually experienced. This may be one in which you feel good about your response, or it may be one in which your response was not effective in deterring an assailant. If the latter, bear in mind that in any situation, people *do* what they know *how* to do and *you* now have skills and resources that you may not have had then. This is *not* an exercise in self-blame. Rather, it is an opportunity for

you to confront a frightening set of circumstances in a way that will leave you feeling empowered and reassured about your ability to produce a different outcome in any similar future situation.

"Partners, be supportive and cooperative."

Note: Offer this option *only* if the practice environment is perceived to be safe and supportive by the students who participate. You may want to have a support person (e.g., a therapist, crisis counselor, etc.) standing by in case this exercise brings up overwhelming feelings of pain or anger.

Student Success Goals

- Completion of the visualization exercise
- Role play of the visualization with a partner

To Decrease Difficulty

- Have students role-play the Continuum of Response more slowly, taking care to address each decision-step thoroughly before moving on to the next.

To Increase Difficulty

- After a pair of students have completed a role play, have them discuss the possible impact on outcome had the defender used different strategies and tactics. Suggest that they repeat the role play, this time with the attacker deviating at will from the fantasized "script." This way, the defender will be required to respond extemporaneously in figuring out how to best deter the assailant.

Evaluation Ideas

In deciding how to evaluate your students, be sure the methods you establish measure performance both of the physical skills and the mental, emotional, and communication skills that are so critical in the application of preventive strategies, such as De-Escalation and Assertiveness/Confrontation. Also measure students' knowledge of the nature, circumstances, stages, and psychodynamics of various forms of aggression.

COMBINING QUALITATIVE AND QUANTITATIVE EVALUATION

Opportunities for qualitative and quantitative evaluation of self-defense knowledge and skills are thoroughly integrated into each step in the participant's book *Self-Defense: Steps to Success.* The Keys to Success provide qualitative objectives for all basic skills, and the Keys to Success Checklists allow for evaluation of these skills by a peer, teacher, or coach. On the other hand, the Success Goals in both the participant's book and the instructor's guide provide a mechanism for *quantitative* assessment of performance.

This combination of both qualitative and quantitative methods of evaluation insures fairness to beginning students, who will be able to match more experienced or athletic students in quantitative measures, despite being perhaps less accomplished in technique. The two methods, of course, are closely related, given that in the process of meeting quantitative objectives (Success Goals), your beginning students' technique should become steadily better (technically more precise, balanced, faster, more powerful and accurate).

The participant's book also features Rating Your Progress, a questionnaire that is generally completed at the end of this course of study. With this self-evaluation tool, your students can rate their own skills and capabilities in all aspects of self-defense.

ADAPTING AN INDIVIDUAL PROGRAM

The Sample Individual Program in Appendix C.1 describes a primarily quantitative assess-ment. (A blank program sheet is also provided in Appendix C.2.) To adapt this evaluation system to your specific situation, determine which skills you will be evaluating, how much weight you will place on any one skill or capability, and the type of grading system you will use, for example, letter grades (D, C, B, A), numbers (1, 2, 3, 4), or simply satisfactory or unsatisfactory, as I have done.

In evaluating performance skills, I generally use satisfactory (1 point) or unsatisfactory (0 point), based on the student's completion of the required repetitions. I try to avoid labeling a student's performance of a particular technique as of "D" quality. Because self-defense involves the learning of life-saving skills, not merely sport skills, qualitative performance evaluations of this sort may only reinforce feelings of powerlessness and incompetence in meeting aggression. Indeed, helping students *overcome* feelings of learned helplessness is a major challenge in teaching self-defense.

Students in my classes do receive a final letter grade, but it is based on the written evaluation, completion of all assigned projects, and meeting of *quantitative* success goals. High quality of skills will be assured by conscientious and careful use of those mechanisms for qualitative evaluation that are built into this course (the Keys to Success and the Keys to Success Checklist) and by their teacher's judicious, appropriate feedback and guidance, especially for students who may be struggling to master these skills.

Evaluate each student on the 12 skills listed in the Sample Individual Program (Appendix C.1). If you must limit the skills you personally evaluate, focus on the foundational skills; that is, evaluate Skills 5, 6, 7, 8, 9, and 10. These responses to various grab attacks incorporate most of the earlier learned skills, such as evasions, blocks, and counterattacks. Also, include De-Escalation and Assertiveness/Confrontation as skills to be evaluated.

I have weighted each of these skills on the basis of difficulty and degree of emphasis in my own classes. You may have other criteria to consider, such as time available for practice, that will suggest further modification.

WRITTEN EXAMINATION

A written examination is included for the purpose of measuring your students' knowledge of the nature, typical circumstances, stages, and psychodynamics of various forms of assaultive or threatening behavior. Because this knowledge is at the heart of effective prevention and postponement of physical aggression, I recommend that it—or a written examination of you own devising—be part of the evaluation of your students.

Test Bank

This section includes 68 questions (worth 80 points) that your students should be able to answer after completing a course using the textbook *Self-Defense: Steps to Success*. Select from these the questions that reflect your emphases in the teaching of these skills, or create questions of your own, using these as models.

FILL IN THE BLANK

Directions: From the following list, fill in the blanks with the word or phrase that best completes the statement. Each is used only once. (29 points)

selection	assertiveness/confrontation	force
counterattack	sexual assault	action
vulnerability	aggravated assault	testing
awareness	breathe deeply and slowly	thumbs
centerline	clearly state expectations	assessment
de-escalation	threatening individual	accessibility
communication	positive self-talk	self-defense
physical mastery	name offensive behavior	yourself
confrontation	ethic of least harm	immediate retreat
physical aggression	the environment	

1. Name the three A's of personal safety.

   _____   _____   _____

2. Which is the form of personal violence where power, anger, and sexuality meet?

   _____

3. In which form of violence is serious bodily injury intended and a weapon used?

   _____

4. What are the two key factors in selection of a potential victim of sexual assault?

   _____ and _____

5. Name three common stages of sexual assault.

   _____   _____   _____

6. In assessing a situation, you would rapidly take in information regarding

   _____ , _____ , and _____ .

7. The four Action strategies presented in this book are _____ ,

   _____ , _____ , and _____ .

8. De-escalation consists of controlling your own emotional state and controlling

   _____ .

9. Two techniques for controlling anxiety and fear in a threatening situation are

   _____ and _____ .

10. The strategy that represents a potential victim's firm and direct refusal to comply with behaviors that a sexual assailant expects from a typical victim is _____ .

11. Two principles governing the verbal response of the potential victim of sexual assault during the testing stage are _____ and _____ .

12. Self-defense is called the strategy of last resort and is used in response to _____ .

13. A commitment to using the least damaging or punishing defense in order to deter an attacker is called the _____ .

14. The 8- to 12-inch-wide zone protected by the guard is called the _____ .

15. The act of responding to an attack with a strike or kick of your own is called a

   _____ .

16. A fundamental principle of wrist releases involves concentrating force against the attacker's

   _____ .

17. The first step in insuring recall of self-defense techniques under stress of an actual assault is

   _____ .

MULTIPLE CHOICE

Directions: Circle the letter of the choice that best completes the statement. Give only one answer. (32 points)

1. The process of quickly and accurately evaluating a potentially assaultive situation is called
   a. awareness
   b assessment
   c. taking precautionary measures
   d. action

2. Which three action strategies are implemented before the onset of physical aggression?
   a. assessment, de-escalation, assertiveness/confrontation
   b immediate retreat, assertiveness/confrontation, de-escalation
   c. awareness, assessment, immediate retreat
   d. evasions, de-escalation, assertiveness/confrontation

3. According to the U.S. Dept. of Justice statistics, how many North Americans will be victims of violent crime, either attempted or completed, at least once in their lives?
   a. 5 out of 6
   b. 1 out of 2
   c. 1 out of 3
   d. 8 out of 10

4. Women and children make up the majority of victims in the area of
   a. simple assault
   b. assault by strangers
   c. family violence
   d. gang violence

5. Harlow (1989) reported that the occupational group having twice the injury rate of other groups from violent victimization was
   a. farmers
   b. service workers
   c. homemakers
   d. door-to-door salespeople

6. Which of the following is a common misconception about sexual assault?
   a. Provocative and seductive dress is a key factor in the selection of victims.
   b. Women seldom bring false charges of rape.
   c. Sexual assailants are motivated by a desire for mastery and conquest.
   d. All of these are common misconceptions.

7. Koss (1985) found that what percentage of women in college have been raped?
   a. 2%
   b. 25%
   c. 40%
   d. 10%

8. Groth and Birnbaum (1979) describe three patterns of sexual assault. What are they?
   a. power rape, anger rape, sadistic rape
   b. power rape, anger rape, casual rape
   c. date rape, stranger rape, gang rape
   d. spontaneous rape, planned rape, sadistic rape

9. Research suggests which of the following is the key factor in deterring unarmed sexual assailants?
   a. passive resistance
   b. immediate and firm resistance
   c. biding one's time and then resisting vigorously
   d. compliance with attacker's demands

10. When assessing the environment in which an attack is threatened, one should note
    a. proximity, positioning, and identity of other people
    b. barriers
    c. avenues of escape
    d. all of these

11. Which of the four action strategies provides the best possible chance of avoiding injury or harm?
    a. immediate retreat
    b. de-escalation
    c. assertiveness/confrontation
    d. self-defense

12. Which of these is *not* a behavior that suggests confidence and attentiveness?
    a. assuming a relaxed, alert posture
    b. avoiding eye contact
    c. assuming a neutral facial experssion
    d. minimizing extraneous movement

13. In positioning yourself for safety, which of these would you do?
    a. maintain a distance of 1 arm's-length
    b. angle your body 90 degrees
    c. keep your arms folded protectively across your chest
    d. all of the above

14. Using observational inquiries, asking open-ended questions, and using encouragers are all examples of
    a. using clear communication
    b. acknowledging feelings
    c. active listening
    d. asserting yourself

15. Which of these is likely to escalate a situation?
    a. finger wagging
    b. ignoring
    c. shouting
    d. all of these

16. Which defusing technique is especially useful when someone or something in the immediate vicinity is contributing to a potential assailant's agitation?
    a. redirect
    b. sit down
    c. change the environment
    d. use humor

17. Which defusing technique involves setting clear conditions for further interaction?
    a. define behavioral limits
    b. get to yes
    c. redirect
    d. reframe

18. Burkhardt and Stanton found that what percentage of college men had used physical restraint to have intercourse with a woman against her will?
    a. 25%
    b. 2%
    c. 11%
    d. 50%

19. Maneuvers that involve removing your body from the line of attack and avoiding physical contact are called
    a. invasions   c. deflections
    b. blocks   d. evasions

20. A distance of 2 arms'-lengths from the assailant is called the
    a. defensive range   c. circle of safety
    b. critical distance zone   d. offensive zone

21. Which of the following is not an element of a defensive stance?
    a. feet placed 1-1/2 shoulder-widths apart   c. guard in place
    b. body angled at 45 degrees   d. hands tightly fisted

22. Which of these is not an element of inside or outside blocking?
    a. maintaining forearm nearly perpendicular   c. deflecting punch upward and away
       to the floor   from face
    b. intercepting punch two-thirds of the way   d. using mirror-image arm
       to the target

23. The ideal vision for monitoring incoming punches is
    a. soft and inclusive   c. hard and focused
    b. penetrating   d. discerning

24. Which of these counterattacks would you be more likely to use if you were face-to-face with an attacker?
    a. palm-heel strike   c. horizontal hammerfist
    b. back kick   d. side stomp kick

25. Which of the following are effects of a kiyai?
    a. increases force and speed of counterattacks   c. startles attacker
    b. mobilizes defender   d. all of these

26. Which block is more easily followed by a front-facing counterattack?
    a. inside block   c. rising block
    b. outside block   d. X-block

27. The proper striking surface for a back kick is
    a. ball of the foot   c. heel
    b. blade edge of the foot   d. arch

28. Which of the following is not an element of a side guard?
    a. arms bent at 90 to 120 degrees   c. both arms resting lightly against the body
    b. trailing arm held diagonally across the   d. hands loosely fisted
       body, shielding the centerline

29. Which of the following is likely to be the most effective response when an attacker you are facing grabs at your throat from a distance of 1 arm's-length?
    a. evasive sidestep   c. duck
    b. flying wedge and push-away   d. run backwards as fast as you can

30. Which of the following is a possible response to a rear choke hold?
    a. head butt with kiyai   c. horizontal hammerfist
    b. elbow jab   d. front snap kick

31. If you are grabbed in a bear hug from behind, which combination counterattack is most likely to be effective?
    a. kick-scrape-heel stomp-head butt   c. head butt-elbow jab-side stomp kick
    b. elbow jab-kick-scrape-heel stomp   d. heel stomp-hammerfist to groin-web strike

32. Another term for preliminary moves used in wrist releases is
    a. distraction technique   c. neutralizing technique
    b. follow-up technique   d. ballistic technique

MATCHING QUESTIONS

Directions: Write the letter of the most appropriate defense for each attack listed. (7 points)

Attacks

____ 1. lunging punch
____ 2. mugger's hold
____ 3. attempted front choke
____ 4. verbal threats from agitated individual
____ 5. wrist grabs
____ 6. verbal intimidation by sexual assailant
____ 7. rear bear hug

Defenses

a. kick-scrape-stomp-head butt
b. de-escalation
c. evasive sidestep
d. quick wrist releases
e. flying wedge-push-away
f. release-elbow-kick
g. assertiveness/confrontation

TRUE OR FALSE QUESTIONS

Directions: Indicate whether each statement is true (T) or false (F) by writing the appropriate letter in the space. (12 points)

____ 1. Women are the exclusive victims of sexual assault.

____ 2. The vast majority of assaults involve one victim and one assailant.

____ 3. Over half of assaults occur in the daytime.

____ 4. Most assaults occur in the vicinity of the attacker's home.

____ 5. Outside of family violence, men are more often victims of assault.

____ 6. Rape is considered to be one of the most underreported of violent crimes, with only an estimated 10% to 30% being reported.

____ 7. Studies have shown that an overwhelming majority of rapists do not differ significantly from the norm in their physical or psychological characteristics, except for a tendency to be more likely to express hostility and frustration.

____ 8. De-escalation refers to verbal and psychological skills used in dealing with a sexual assailant motivated by a desire for dominance.

____ 9. Koss found that date rapists are frequently sexually aggressive men who oversubscribe to traditional male roles and believe that aggression is normal.

____ 10. Evasions are neutralizing techniques used in responding to attacks initiated from inside the critical distance zone.

____ 11. The primary purpose of impact drills is to be able to practice full-power, full-speed technique against a bag.

____ 12. If an attacker secures a stranglehold, loss of consciousness will result in approximately 60 seconds.

WRITTEN EXAMINATION ANSWERS

Fill in the Blank:

1. awareness, assessment, action
2. sexual assault
3. aggravated assault
4. vulnerability, accessibility
5. selection, testing, force
6. the environment, threatening individual, yourself
7. immediate retreat, de-escalation, assertiveness/confrontation, self-defense
8. communication
9. breathe deeply and slowly, positive self-talk
10. confrontation
11. name offensive behavior, clearly state expectations
12. physical aggression
13. ethic of least harm
14. centerline
15. counterattack
16. thumbs
17. physical mastery

Multiple Choice:

1. b
2. b
3. a
4. c
5. b
6. a
7. b
8. a
9. b
10. d
11. a
12. b
13. b
14. c
15. d
16. c
17. a
18. c
19. d
20. b
21. d
22. c
23. a
24. a
25. d
26. b
27. c
28. c
29. b
30. b
31. a
32. a

Matching:

1. c
2. f
3. e
4. b
5. d
6. g
7. a

True or False:

1. F
2. T
3. F
4. F
5. T
6. T
7. T
8. F
9. T
10. F
11. F
12. F

Appendix A
How to Use the Knowledge Structure Overview

A knowledge structure is an instructional tool. By completing one you make a very personal statement about what you know about a subject and how that knowledge guides your decisions in teaching. The knowledge structure for self-defense outlined here has been designed for a teaching environment, with teaching progressions that emphasize technique and performance objectives in realistic settings.

The Knowledge Structure of Self-Defense shows the first page or an overview of a completed knowledge structure. The knowledge structure is divided into broad categories of information that are used for all of the participant and instructor guides in the Steps to Success Activity Series. Those categories are

- physiological training and conditioning,
- background knowledge,
- psychomotor skills and strategies, and
- psychosocial concepts.

Physiological training and conditioning has several subcategories, including warm-up, conditioning, and cool-down. Research in exercise physiology and the medical sciences has demonstrated the importance of warming up and cooling down after physical activity. The participant and instructor guides present principles and exercises for effective warm-up and cool-down. They also present minimal strength-building exercises for conditioning the upper torso, necessary preparation for effective execution of the upper body techniques presented in this text.

Background knowledge outlines essential knowledge that all instructors should command when meeting their classes. For self-defense, background knowledge includes awareness of the nature, circumstances, stages, and psychodynamics of various forms of interpersonal aggression; assessment of specific situational factors; preventive strategies; and legal and ethical issues in the use of self-defense.

Under psychomotor skills and strategies, all the individual skills in an activity are named. For self-defense, these are shown as neutralizing techniques, such as evasive sidestep, inside and outside blocks, and circling retreat. (Neutralizing techniques, such as hold breaks and flying wedges, are integrated into "Applications and Adaptations.") Other individual skills are counterattacks, including punches, eye gouges, palm-heel strikes, web strikes, front snap kicks, elbow jabs, back kicks, scrapes and stomps, and head butts. These skills are presented in a recommended order of presentation. In a completed knowledge structure, each skill is broken down into subskills, delineating selected technical, biomechanical, motor learning, and other teaching and coaching points that describe mature performance. These points can be found in the Keys to Success and the Keys to Success Checklists in the participant book.

Once individual skills are identified and analyzed, the selected basic tactics of the activity are also identified and analyzed. These tactics include the application of the basic skills to defenses against common grab attacks, such as the attempted front choke hold, secured front choke hold, mugger's hold, bear hug, and three variations of the wrist grab.

The psychosocial category identifies selected concepts from the sport psychology and sociology literature that have been shown to contribute to the learners' understanding of and success in the activity. These concepts are built into the key concepts and activities for teaching. For self-defense, the concepts identified are empowerment, recall under stress, de-escalation, and assertiveness.

To be a successful teacher, you must convert what you have learned and practiced as a student to knowledge that is conscious and appropriate for presentation to others. A knowledge structure is a tool designed to help you accomplish this and to speed your steps to success. You should view a knowledge structure as the most basic level of teaching knowledge you possess for a sport or activity. For more information on how to develop your own knowledge structure, see the textbook that accompanies this series, *Instructional Design for Teaching Physical Activities* (Vickers, 1990).

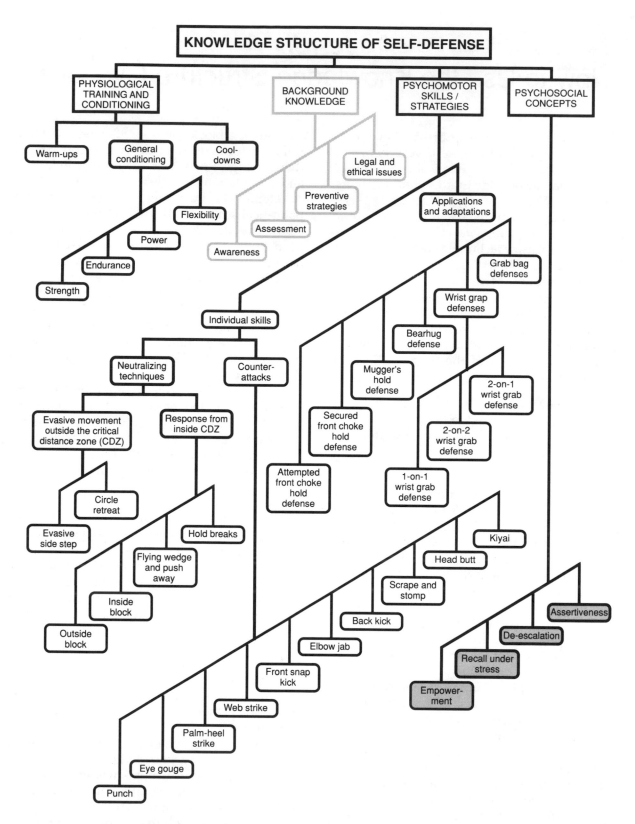

Note. From "The Role of Expert Knowledge Structures in an Instructional Design Model for Physical Education" by J.N. Vickers, 1983, *Journal of Teaching in Physical Education*, **2**(3), pp. 25, 27. Copyright 1983 by Joan N. Vickers. Adapted by permission. This Knowledge Structure of Self-Defense was designed specifically for the Steps to Success Activity Series by Joan N. Vickers, Judy P. Wright, and Joan M. Nelson.

Appendix B.1
How to Use the Scope and Teaching Sequence Form

A completed Scope and Teaching Sequence is, in effect, a master lesson plan. It lists all the individual skills to be included in your course, recorded (vertically) in the progressive sequence in which you have decided to present them and showing (horizontally) the manner and the sessions in which you teach them.

The Sample Scope and Teaching Sequence illustrates how the chart is to be used. This chart indicates that in Session 1, you will introduce the 3 A's (thoroughly covering Awareness and Assessment, while simply pointing out the three Action strategies) and then introducing the evasive sidestep. Drills in Step 1 (Awareness) and Step 2 (Assessment) are given as homework assignments, designated by the letter H and a number corresponding to the drill number. Time is then allotted for students to report back during specific sessions (e.g., results of Drill 1, Awareness (H/1) are discussed in the third session, following continued (C) practice of evasive sidesteps and review (R) of blocks).

Note that although it is mentioned in Session 1, De-escalation is covered in depth for the first time during Sessions 13 and 14 and reviewed later during Session 24. Assertiveness/Confron-tation is presented in detail during Session 19 and reviewed during Session 26. Review of both of these Action strategies might consist of quickly recalling the nonverbal and verbal principles of each and then practicing these in a role play.

A course Scope and Teaching Sequence chart (use the blank form in Appendix B.2) will help you to better plan your daily teaching strategies (see Appendix D). It will take some experience to predict accurately how much material you can cover in each session, but by completing a plan like this, you can compare your progress to your plan and revise the plan to better fit the next class. The chart will also help you tailor the amount of material to the length of time you have to teach it. Be sure that your course's Scope and Teaching Sequence allots ample time for review and practice of each area.

Remember that the Scope and Teaching Sequence can be affected by the number of students in a class and the collective abilities of your students. Though the one presented here or the one you complete for yourself can serve as a guide, it is very difficult to follow any plan exactly. Be ready to make adjustments as your conditions warrant them.

Sample Scope and Teaching Sequence

New [N]   Review [R]   Continue [C]   Homework reports [H]   De-escalation [D]   Assertiveness/Confrontation [A]

NAME OF ACTIVITY   Self-Defense _____

LEVEL OF LEARNER _____

Steps	Session Number	1	2	3	4	5	6	7	8	9	10	11	12	13	14	15	16	17	18	19	20	21	22	23	24	25	26	27	28	29	30
	Introduction/Orientation	N																													
1	Awareness	N		H$_1$		H$_2$																									
2	Assessment	N						H$_1$		H$_2$		H$_3$																			
3	Action	N											N/D	C/D					N/A						R/D		R/A				
4	Evasive sidestep		N	R	C		C	C	C	C					C		C				C		C			C		C			
5	Blocks			N	R	C	C	C	C	C							C				C		C			C		C			
6	Front-facing counterattacks				N	R	C	C	C	C							C				C		C			C		C			
7	Rear-directed counterattacks							N	R	C								C				C				C		C			
8	Side-directed counterattacks									N	R	C												C		C					
9	Response to attempted front choke												N		R		C				C		C			C		C			
10	Response to secured front choke																N	R		C		C				C		C			
11	Response to mugger's hold																		N	R		C				C		C			
12	Response to rear bear hug																				N	R		C		C		C			
13	Response to wrist grabs																							N	R		C				
14	Recall under stress																											N	R	C	
	Written exam																														N

Notes:

Appendix B.2

Scope and Teaching Sequence

NAME OF ACTIVITY _____

LEVEL OF LEARNER _____

New [N] Review [R] Continue [C] Homework reports [H] De-escalation [D] Assertiveness/Confrontation [A]

Session Number	1	2	3	4	5	6	7	8	9	10	11	12	13	14	15	16	17	18	19	20	21	22	23	24	25	26	27	28	29	30
Steps																														

Appendix C.1
How to Use the Individual Program Form

To complete an individual program for each student, you must first make five decisions about evaluation:

1. How many skills or concepts can you or should you evaluate, considering the number of students and the time available? The larger your classes and the shorter your class length, the fewer objectives you will be able to use.
2. What specific quantitative or qualitative criteria will you use to evaluate specific skills? See the Sample Individual Program for ideas.
3. What relative weight is to be assigned to each specific skill, considering its importance in the course and the amount of practice time available?
4. What type of grading system do you wish to use? Will you use letters (A, B, C, D), satisfactory/unsatisfactory, a number or point system (1, 2, 3, etc.), or percentages? Or, do you prefer a system of achievement levels such as colors (red, white, blue), creatures (panthers, lions, tigers), or medallions (bronze, silver, gold)?
5. Who will do the evaluating? You may want to delegate certain quantitative evaluations to be made by the students' peers up to a predetermined skill level (e.g., a "B" grade), with all qualitative evaluations and all top-grade determinations being made by you.

When you have made these decisions, draw up an evaluation sheet (using Appendix C.2) that will fit the majority of your class members. Then decide whether you will establish a minimum level as a passing/failing point. Calculate the minimum passing score and the maximum attainable score, and divide the difference into as many grade categories as you wish. If you use an achievement-level system, assign a numerical value to each level.

The blank Individual Program form, shown in Appendix C.2, is intended not to be used verbatim (although you may do so, if you wish), but rather to suggest ideas that you can use, adapt, and integrate with your own ideas to tailor your program to you and your students.

Make copies of your program evaluation system to hand out to each student at your first class meeting, and be prepared to make modifications for those who need special consideration. Such modifications could include changing the weight assigned to particular skills for certain students, substituting some skills for others, or varying the criteria used for evaluating selected students. Thus, individual differences can be recognized within your class.

You, the instructor, have the freedom to make the decisions about evaluating your students. Be creative. The best teachers always are.

Sample Individual Program

Individual course in _____Self-Defense_____   Grade/Course section _____

Student's name _____   Student ID # _____

Skills/concepts	Technique and performance objectives	WT*	Point × progress** = Unsatisfactory = 0	Satisfactory = 2	Final score***
1 Defensive stance	Body angled 45 degrees, weight evenly distributed over 1-1/2-shoulder-width stance, spine erect, knees bent, guard up	1.0			
2 Evasions	*Technique:* Explosive step to side at last moment, followed by quick step forward and out of range *Performance:* Minimum of 25 in each direction	1.5			
3 Blocks	*Technique:* Rotation of trunk in direction of block, mirror image, elbow bent at 90 degrees, forearm perpendicular, intercept wrist-to-wrist when punch is 2/3 of way to target *Performance:* Minimum of 100 repetitions of both outside and inside block	2.0			
4 Counterattacks	*Technique:* Rotation of trunk to launch technique, correct trajectories, correct striking surfaces and accurate targeting, appropriate hand/foot position, penetration *Performance:* Minimum of 30 repetitions of each counterattack (front-facing, rear-directed, side-directed) to each side	2.5			
5 Response to attempted front choke hold	*Technique:* Explosive movement of vertical forearms to either side, rotation to palm-out position, wrist-to-wrist interception, striking surface on little-finger edge, deflection of attacker's arms to either side *Performance:* 75 repetitions of progressively more realistic defenses	2.0			
6 Response to secured front choke hold	*Technique:* Attacker's wrists grabbed firmly, kick delivered precisely to knee, rechambered leg, wide plant, correctly executed and powerful flying wedge, precisely targeted palm-heel strike to nose *Performance:* 140 repetitions with variable emphasis (see Drills)	2.5			

(continued)

Sample Individual Program (continued)

Skills/concepts	Technique and performance objectives	WT* ×	Point progress** Unsatisfactory = 0	Satisfactory = 2	Final score***
7 Response to mugger's hold	*Technique:* Attacker's forearm grabbed below elbow and wrist, defender's elbows lifted; attacker's forearm rolled down; defender's chin dropped, and attacker's hands pinned to chest, then elbow jab to ribs/solar plexus, back kick to knee/shin *Performance:* 75 repetitions with variable emphasis (see Drills)	2.5			
8 Response to rear bear hug	*Technique:* Balance maintained, targets sighted; kick chambered and heel driven into target, shin scrape with blade edge, heel stomp to attacker's instep, head butt to attacker's nose *Performance:* 35 repetitions with variable emphasis (see Drills); improvisation of defenses in response to unfamiliar rear grabs	2.5			
9 Response to wrist grabs	*Technique:* Fist trapped hand(s), grasp firmly with free hand, straight wrist lines, force directed against attacker's thumb(s), trunk rotation, kiyais *Performance:* 15 repetitions each of releases for 1-on-1, 2-on-2, 2-on-1 grabs; 50 repetitions of releases preceded by distraction techniques; 40 repetitions of releases with follow-up techniques; 40 repetitions of combination of distraction-wrist release-follow up.	2.0			
10 Recall under stress	Concentration, focus, accurate observations, ability to adjust to changes in positioning and range, disciplined and effective application of technique, calm in the face of threat or aggression	3.0			
11 De-escalation	Correct application of nonverbal and verbal principles in role-play situations. Minimum of 12 points in role play (see *Self-Defense,* Step 3, De-Escalation Drill 3)	2.5			
12 Assertiveness/ confrontation	Correct application of nonverbal and verbal principles in role-play situations. Minimum of 15 points in role play (see *Self-Defense,* Step 3, Assertiveness/ Confrontation Drills 1 and 2)	2.5			

*WT = Weighting of an objective's degree of difficulty.

**Progress = Ongoing success, which may be expressed in terms of (a) accumulated points (1, 2, 3, 4); (b) grades (D, C, B, A); (c) symbols (merit, bronze, silver, gold); (d) unsatisfactory/satisfactory; and others as desired.

***Final score = WT × Progress.

Appendix C.2

Individual Program

Individual course in _____   Grade/Course section _____

Student's name _____   Student ID # _____

Skills/concepts	Technique and performance objectives	WT*	×	Point progress**	=	Final score***
				Unsatisfactory = 0	Satisfactory = 2	

(continued)

Individual Program (continued)

*WT = Weighting of an objective's degree of difficulty.

**Progress = Ongoing success, which may be expressed in terms of (a) accumulated points (1, 2, 3, 4); (b) grades (D, C, B, A); (c) symbols (merit, bronze, silver, gold); (d) unsatisfactory/satisfactory; and others as desired.

***Final score = WT × Progress.

Appendix D.1
How to Use the Lesson Plan Form

All teachers have learned during their training that lesson plans are vital to good teaching. An organized, professional approach to teaching requires preparing daily lesson plans. This is a commonly accepted axiom, but there are many variations in the *form* that lesson plans can take. (Appendix D.2 presents a blank Lesson Plan form that you may modify to fit your own needs.)

Generally, a lesson plan provides an effective overview of your intended instruction in sufficient detail that following it will allow someone else to teach your class in your absence. But, an *effective* lesson plan also sets forth the objectives to be attained or attempted during the session. If there are no objectives, then there is no reason for teaching, and no basis for judging whether the teaching is effective. So, always begin your lesson plan with a statement (or list) of the skills you want your students to achieve by the end of that particular class period.

When you have named your objectives, list specific activities that will lead to attaining each. Describe each activity in detail—what will take place and in what order, and how the class will be organized for the optimum learning situation. Record key words or phrases as focal points, as well as brief reminders of the applicable safety precautions (e.g., tell your students to stop short of contact, move slowly during early repetitions, allow 4 to 6 feet of space between pairs, etc.).

Finally, to guide you in keeping to your plan, set a time schedule that allocates a segment of the class period for each activity. Also include in your lesson plan a list of all the teaching and safety equipment you will need, as well as a reminder to check the availability and location of the equipment before class.

Sample Lesson Plan

Lesson Plan __3__ of __30__

Activity _____Self-Defense_____

Class _____1:00-1:50 pm_____

Equipment _____None_____

_____

_____

Objectives: 1. Student will do 25 evasive sidesteps in each direction, in response to attacker-initiated charges. 2. Student will do 150 repetitions each of outside and inside blocks in response to predictable and unpredictable punch attacks. 3. Students will share and discuss results of their Self-Study of Precautionary Measures.

Skill or concept	Learning activities	Teaching points	Time
Outline objectives			1 min
Warm-up	Preliminary phase	Mild aerobic exercise	3 min
	Flexibility exercises	Stretch slowly	6 min
	Strength-building exercises	Do correctly, gradually increase repetitions	8 min
Evasive sidestep	Triangle Drill (Step 4, Drill 2)	Spine erect, explosive move, correct timing	5 min
	Triangle Drill With Spontaneous Attacks (Step 4, Drill 4)	Monitoring, quick movement, timely reaction, correct form under stress	5 min
Punches	Predictable Punch Drill (Step 5, Drill 2)	Correct execution, timely interception	5 min
	Unpredictable Punch Drill (Step 5, Drill 4)	Effective monitoring, mirror-image blocks	5 min
	Variable Block Drill (Step 5, Drill 6)	Monitoring, note angle & likely follow-up, easy mixing of outside and inside blocks	5 min
Cool-down	Stretches	Slowly, gently	2 min
Awareness of precautionary measures	Sharing results and discussion of Self-Study (Step 1, Drill 1)	Be selective, blend into life patterns, keep in mind goal to increase security & not to limit choices/life	5 min

Appendix D.2

Lesson Plan

Lesson plan _____ of _____   Objectives:

Activity _____

Class _____

Equipment _____

_____

_____

Skill or concept	Learning activities	Teaching points	Time

Note: From *Badminton: A Structures of Knowledge Approach* (p. 95) by J.N. Vickers and D. Brecht, 1987, Calgary, AB: University Printing Services. Copyright 1987 by Joan N. Vickers. Adapted by permission.

References

Burkhart, B., & Stanton, A. (1988). Sexual aggression in acquaintance relationships. In G. Russell (Ed.), *Violence in intimate relationships* (pp. 43-65). Great Neck, NY: PMA.

Goc-Karp, G., & Zakrajsek, D.B. (1987). Planning for learning: Theory into practice. *Journal of Teaching in Physical Education*, **6**(4), 377-392.

Housner, L.D., & Griffey, D.C. (1985). Teacher cognition: Differences in planning and interactive decision making between experienced and inexperienced teachers. *Research Quarterly for Exercise and Sport*, **56**(1), 45-53.

Imwold, C.H., & Hoffman, S.J. (1983). Visual recognition of a gymnastic skill by experienced and inexperienced instructors. *Research Quarterly for Exercise and Sport*, **54**(2), 149-155.

Koss, M. (1985, October). Ms. magazine campus project on sexual assault. [Funded by National Center for the Prevention and Control of Rape]. *Ms.*, p. 58.

Vickers, J.N. (1990). *Instructional Design for Teaching Physical Activities*. Champaign, IL: Human Kinetics Publishers.

About the Author

As an instructor of self-defense and a fourth-degree black belt, Joan M. Nelson has over 20 years of active training in martial arts and was recently inducted into the Michigan Karate Hall of Fame. She received her master's degree in health and physical education from Michigan State University and is the founder and owner of Movement Arts, Inc., a Lansing-based consulting firm offering training and education programs in conflict management and self-defense as well as health and fitness-related services.

Specializing in the prevention of workplace violence, Nelson has served as a consultant in personal safety skills training for a variety of public and private sector groups, including the Michigan Department of Corrections and western European self-defense instructors. She is a cofounder of the National Women's Martial Arts Federation, a member of The American Society of Training and Development, and an active participant in antiviolence groups.